Understanding
WINE

A Guide to Winetasting and Wine Appreciation

THE SIMON & SCHUSTER
BEGINNER'S GUIDE TO
Understanding
WINE

By Michael Schuster

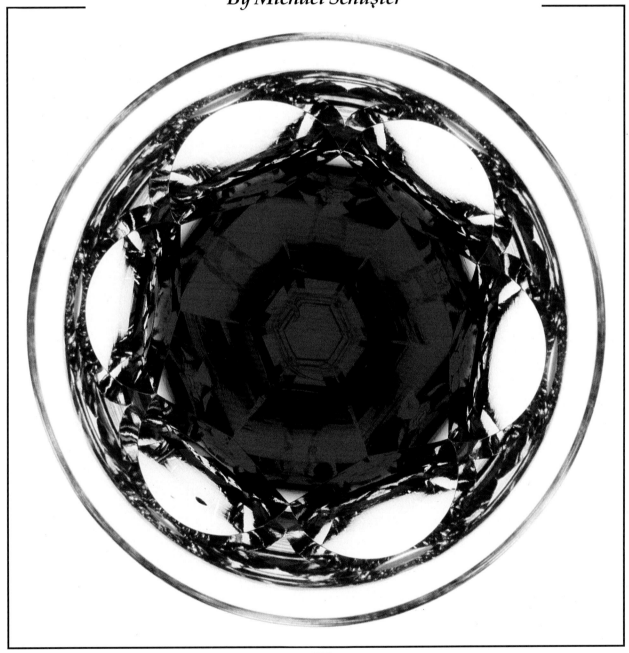

A Fireside Book
Published by Simon & Schuster Inc.
New York   London   Toronto   Sydney   Tokyo   Singapore

To Karen
for all her love and encouragement

FIRESIDE
Simon & Schuster Building
Rockefeller Centre
1230 Avenue of the Americas
New York, New York 10020

First published in Great Britain in 1989
by Mitchell Beazley International Ltd.
Artists House, 14-15 Manette Street,
London W1V 5LB

Edited and designed by the Artists House Division
of Mitchell Beazley International Ltd.

Library of Congress Cataloging in Publication Data
Schuster, Michael.
(Understanding wine)
The Simon & Schuster beginner's guide to
understanding wine/by Michael Schuster.
    p.   cm.
Previously published as: Understanding wine.
"A Fireside book."
Includes index.
ISBN 0-671-72893-8
1. Wine and wine making. I. Title. II. Title: Simon and
Schuster beginner's guide to understanding wine.
TP548.S462 1990
641.2'2 – dc20

Art Editor: *Hans Verkroost*
Designer: *Ruth Levy*
Editor: *Alison Franks*
Production: *Peter Phillips, Stewart Bowling*

Typeset by Hourds Typographica, Stafford
Color reproduction by La Cromolito s.n.c. Milan
Printed in Portugal by Printer Portuguesa Grafica Lda.

10 9 8 7 6 5 4 3 2 1

ISBN: 0-671-72893-8

Contents

INTRODUCTION

This book is for beginners and seasoned wine tasters alike. In particular it is for those of you who, like me, have become endlessly curious about wines themselves and how to enjoy them to the utmost. It is full of my own enthusiasms and, no doubt, my prejudices, too; but if it fires you with any of my early passion for the subject or perhaps provokes you to reconsider a cherished view, then I will feel it has been worthwhile.

My own interest was awakened relatively late. A farm in the Kenya highlands was hardly the ideal place for early exposure to good wine. My mother was practically teetotal, my father's alcoholic diet was mainly Tusker Lager and it was left to an uncle and a close friend to introduce me to its pleasures — one with a present of twenty-five good bottles and the other with a copy of Hugh Johnson's *Wine* — both for my twenty-fifth birthday. There was no conspiracy to convert, but had there been it could not have been more successful.

My conversion proceeded almost literally with the book in one hand and a glass in the other. Before opening a bottle I read the appropriate section to see what I might expect, and then I smelled and sipped the reality already primed with words and analogies that both revealed the wine's tastes and helped convey my enjoyment. As a hedonist who derives as much sensual pleasure from language as from fragrance and flavour, the combination was irresistible!

Subsequently, for a more disciplined approach to tasting, I am indebted both to Michael Broadbent's book *Wine Tasting* and, having first taken his Tasting Diploma in Bordeaux and then translated his book *Le Goût du Vin*, to Emile Peynaud.

But however much a book can convey, there is no better way of learning about wines than by actually tasting with experienced and articulate tasters; and, for their enthusiasm, perceptive criticism, and generosity with bottles, time and knowledge, I owe a great deal to Leslie Simon and Steven Schneider.

I also want to thank the publishing team at Mitchell Beazley: Kelly Flynn for asking me to write this book in the first place, Alison Franks for her gentle editing, the design team of Hans Verkroost and Ruth Levy for their visual creativity, and finally Susan Egerton-Jones for her seemingly endless patience when I failed to meet (impossible) deadlines.

The book is divided into three parts, and, although it is organized in a logical sequence and can be read as a "course", there is no need to start at the beginning as almost any section will be quite comprehensible on its own so that the book can just as easily be used as a reference volume.

TASTING TECHNIQUES is the "how to do it" section. It shows you how to make the most effective use of your senses, describes the actual mechanics of tasting, covers words and making notes, and explains why wines taste the way they do.

Having said earlier that you don't need to start at the beginning, even the most seasoned tasters do well to review their technique from time to time, thus a look at the pages covering The Senses is probably in order for everyone!

GRAPES AND THEIR WINES describes how red and white wines are made and how this affects their taste, and then goes on to the wines themselves, approached by grape variety rather than country and region. For each major grape variety I have tried to illustrate what its wines from around the world have in common as well as their diversity of styles and qualities. As the grape variety approach does not work for sparkling and fortified wines, nor for spirits, each of these has a separate section describing their manufacture, various characteristics and how to taste them.

Grapes and their Wines can be read, glass in hand, to see what to expect from and what you should look for in any particular wine, or it can be used to plan a tasting which will demonstrate the varying guises of any grape in wines from around the globe. If you don't know where to turn because you don't know the grape variety of your wine, then first look up its name at the end of the book in the Wine to Grape Index.

THE PRACTICAL REFERENCE makes up the final part of the book, guiding you through blind tasting, then dealing with the practical matters of handling, serving and storing wine. Finally, it contains The Wine to Grapes Index, which will enable you to identify the grape variety(s) in a wine that you may only know by a place name, and a Glossary.

Michael Schuster

WINE TASTING TECHNIQUES

Knowing how to taste and what to expect from different wines will enhance your enjoyment of them.

GLASSES

Why do winetasters make such a fuss about glasses? The answer is that when "tasting" consciously as opposed to just "drinking", one is trying to experience as many as possible of the sight, smell and taste sensations that a wine has to offer. Smell especially, because it is so central to the pleasure a wine gives and because it conveys so much information. The extent to which one can experience a wine's visual aspect and its smell in particular, is influenced respectively by the quality of the glass it is made from and by the shape of the glass.

Try comparing a line up of different glasses like those illustrated.

All of these glasses are perfectly good as drinking vessels. Only a couple are good for both seeing the wine clearly *and* smelling it effectively; most do neither very well, Why so?

DEPTH AND CLARITY (viewed from above)
When each glass is filled with what would be an average tasting sample of about 35cl of the same wine, and the wine is viewed from directly above to assess its depth and clarity, only in glasses 1 and 2, both with a high lead crystal content, can you really see the wine well. In the cut glass (6), the reflected highlights are splendid but make it difficult to judge the wine's depth. The Paris goblet's breadth dilutes the colour, the sherry copita's narrowness exaggerates it, and in both of these, as well as in glasses 3 and 7, the combination of design and quality of the glass material makes the colour appear flat and uniform. As the photograph shows, the International Standards Organization (ISO) glass gives much the best view of both depth and clarity, though the Classic glass is a close second.

HUE AND NUANCE (viewed with the glass tilted)
Tilting the glass "spreads" the wine so that its overall hue can be seen more clearly (particularly in red wines), as well as the nuances of colour as they change from the centre or "eye" to a watery rim. For this to be practical one must be able to tilt the glass substantially without fear of the wine spilling, and without the rim of the glass then interfering with one's vision. With the flared glasses (6 and 7), the danger of spillage is obvious when tilting to examine colour, or when swirling in order to look at the wine's viscosity or to encourage its bouquet. With the shorter glasses (4 and 5) there simply isn't much room

to either tilt or swirl before the liquid reaches the rim and spills over, and the rim of the glass also remains in the way when viewing. The more "tulip" shaped glasses (1, 2 and 3) are all good "tilters".

BOUQUET
Much more important than their practicality for looking at the wine though, is the way in which the glass affects a wine's smell.

The wider and more flared the glass's opening the less the wine's bouquet will be gathered, concentrated and directed; and the more (and more rapidly) it will disperse and escape via routes other than your nostrils. 1, 3 and 5 would all seem to be good in this

ISO

1

"Classic"
range

2

respect. I say seem, because although they all have a narrow opening, in the case of the sherry copita (5), there is little room for swirling to begin with, little surface area inside for volatization, and barely any room for the bouquet to gather and develop in anyway. Glass (3) is good, but rather too wide at the rim. There is plenty of room for the bouquet to develop on swirling, but it also escapes too easily. A counsel of perfection? Maybe, but the ISO tasting glass is the most efficient all round tasting glass, at a reasonable price, and if you want to get the most out of your wines. ... I also think it is a perfectly good glass for the table, although the range of Classic glasses (2) is hard to beat for appearance and feel.

The extent to which a wine releases its aromas, and how efficiently they can be smelled from the glass depends on four principal, and inter-related factors:
1. The *shape* of the glass.
2. The *surface area inside* on which the wine can be spread by swirling or agitation, allowing the liquid to evaporate and the aroma molecules to volatize.
3. The *space inside* between the surface of the wine at rest and the rim of the glass, in which the aromas have room to circulate, develop and concentrate.
4. The *size of the glass's* opening in relation to the bowl. This must create a fine balance between permitting the aromas to escape and preventing them from doing so.

| Oval claret 3 | Paris goblet 4 | Sherry copita 5 | Cut crystal 6 | Semi-Cut goblet 7 |

(**Left**) *Any of these glasses is practical for drinking, but the combination of design and glass quality does make a noticeable difference to how well you can examine the colour and appearance of the wine from above and with the glass tilted, and to how effectively its bouquet is conveyed.*

Flared glasses (6 & 7) are impractical for swirling the wine to enhance the bouquet or tilting the glass to see the rim colours; they also dissipate the bouquet rather than "gathering" it. You can't help admiring the beautiful stained glass window effect offered by the cut crystal though!

Tulip shaped or inward curving glasses (1–5) allow you to swirl, tilt and get at the bouquet more effectively.

VOCABULARY

Clarity and brightness
muddy
cloudy
bitty
hazy
dull
clear
bright
brilliant
lustrous

Viscosity
viscous
heavy
oily
thin
watery

CO2
bubbles on the glass
bubbles at the rim
bubbles on or just under
   the wine's surface
rising bubbles
pétillant
pearly

*(**Right**) Crystals of tartrate sticking to the bottom of a red wine cork (and dyed purple) and a white wine cork. Occasionally such crystals form a sediment in white wines, notably in old German wines. They are quite harmless and usually indicate that the wine has been stored in cold conditions. Their tartaric acid origin is clear if you taste them.*

THE SENSES: SIGHT

APPEARANCE

Our eyes are the least important of our senses where winetasting is concerned. Although a lustrous, mature wine is a pleasure to look at, one's enjoyment of such a wine would hardly be marred as a blind person, whereas it certainly would be if you had lost your sense of smell. But of course appearance matters. If only because we tend to judge what we are about to eat or drink with our eyes initially, and usually with very clear preconceptions. Milk looks good if it is white and opaque; fresh orange juice needs to be fairly thick and full of solids from the fruit's segments to look appetizing. We want our wine to be clear, bright, and free of sediment to have any appeal.

There is no need to spend much time examining a wine's appearance unless you are blind tasting, in which case colour can yield much information. A glance will tell you whether the wine is clear and bright, but quality of appearance is linked to quality of bouquet and taste. Clarity is simply the absence of any matter in suspension which renders the wine hazy, cloudy, or in any way murky. A lack of clarity is a warning sign. The wine may be out of condition, suffering from a biochemical malady (fairly rare), in which case it will probably smell and taste unpleasant as well; or it may have had a fine deposit which has been shaken back into the wine by careless handling prior to serving.

At ten years the 1976 Sauternes (opp.) had a fine sediment in the bottle. The photographs compare this wine served carefully (poured with care or after decanting), and served carelessly so that its deposit has partly gone back into solution. Not only does the wine containing the sediment look less attractive and indeed less enticing, but its bouquet and flavour will be less refined, less pure, and its texture less glossy, the fine deposit giving it a palpably coarser feel.

Prove this to yourself with a bottle of red wine which has thrown a deposit. After ensuring the deposit has had time to settle completely, compare wine decanted clear from the top half of the bottle with that from the bottom half of the bottle after it has been shaken up. The difference in appearance is obvious; the difference in smell, taste and texture is clear even when tried blindfold. An old bottle of dry or sweet white wine will demonstrate the same thing but will probably be much more expensive.

Brightness is a function of both acidity and of a wine's quality. A wine may be clear and yet not bright, and a wine that is dull to look at will probably

taste dull too, usually because it lacks acidity. This could be the case with a *young* wine made from grapes that had seen too much sunshine, more likely it will be a wine that is just getting old and tired, whatever its quality level.

Brilliance, as distinct from brightness, is a quality factor and the finest wines always seem to have an extra lustre. Simple wines, while not actually "dull" in

10

nothing sinister about this. At the visible level, with a few bubbles clinging to the walls of the glass or hanging just under the surface of the wine, their prickle on the tongue provides an added degree of freshness to many a white and a few reds which are meant to be drunk young, most of which come from warm climates where the natural acidity may be lacking. Indeed, once the bubbles have disappeared in these wines they are losing freshness and they are often past their best. Fine carbon dioxide bubbles rising in a mature, classic red wine would probably indicate an undesirable secondary fermentation, but this is extremely rare today.

Viscosity: "legs", "tears", "arches" and so on. Having given your glass a swirl so that the wine rises up the glass, some of the liquid will cling to the sides after the wine has settled, gathering to form droplets which then run back down the sides. The heavier or more viscous the wine is, either from a high degree of alcohol and/or a high proportion of natural sugar remaining in the wine after fermentation, the more of these "tears" there will be and the longer they will take to form. However, as the way in which they form depends at least as much on the surface of your glass and how clean it is, they are a not very reliable guide to a wine's weight or viscosity — your palate is.

COLOUR

Most of us find it difficult to describe colour accurately. For this reason it is always easier to assess

appearance will tend to look rather plain.

Sediment may also be present in wines that are clear and bright. If this is the case, and the particles haven't marred the appearance of the wine after pouring, they will not mar the taste either, because they are most probably tartrate crystals which are no longer soluble. These are white sugar-like crystals in white wines, purple in red wines, crunchy and slightly acidic to taste, just the same as the cream of tartar on your kitchen shelf, although this is generally ground finer — and they are quite harmless. They are formed from the tartaric acid in the wine, usually as a result of the bottles having been stored in particularly cold conditions, and they can sometimes be seen sticking to the bottom of corks as well.

Carbon dioxide, a natural by-product of fermentation, is present in all wines, although in still wines its presence can rarely be seen or felt. We expect to see its telltale bubbles in sparkling wines, but they are sometimes also visible in "still" wines. There is

(**Left**) *This shows the same wine, the same period of time after swirling, but in two different glasses! The left hand glass was poorly rinsed after washing and the alcohol "tears" are much less pronounced. The point is that "tears" and "arches" are an unreliable guide to a wine's body or weight as much will depend on the interior surface of the glass. Your palate is a surer judge.*

(**Below**) *Fine white wines, mature Burgundy, Graves and Sauternes for example, often throw a very fine deposit. If this is not allowed to settle well, or if the wine is poured without considerable care, it can mar appearance, bouquet and taste almost as much as in an old red wine. This is clear to see in the 1976 Sauternes photographed here.*

Where to look With the
glass tilted there are two
colour sections to describe: the
rim and the "eye" or "bowl".

Rim edge (always watery)

Rim proper which extends
from the watery edge to the
main body of colour. The rim
may be only a few mm wide
($\frac{1}{10}$ of an inch or so) in a
young, concentrated wine, or a
cm ($\frac{1}{2}$ an inch) and more in a
light or mature wine.

Eye or **bowl**, the main body
of colour.

(**Right**) Examining a wine in
a tilted wine glass is the best
way to see its subtleties and
variations of colour. The
differences between the hue
and intensity of colour in the
"eye" and the "rim" are what
to look for. In a red wine the
colour of the rim will give you
some indication of the wine's
age and/or readiness to drink;
in young or immature wines it
will still be purplish, but as
the wines age and mature the
rim will become wider, paler
and increasingly brown-red to
brick coloured.

colour in wines if you have two or more to compare, providing a reference point for both depth and hue. These are the two aspects of colour to look at: depth or intensity refers to the degree of colour; dark red or pale red, for example. Hue refers to the colour properly speaking: red, yellow, gold and so on.

Depth is first examined from directly above, and then with the wineglass tilted. Hue appears relatively uniform and difficult to define when viewed from above, and is much easier to see with the glass tilted and the wine viewed against a plain white background.

What colour tells you *Red wines* lose colour as they age, gradually changing from the purple hues of youth through dark-red, ruby, brown-red, mahogany, to the orange, brick and amber tinted reds of maturity and old age. *White wines* gain in colour as they age, moving from the green-tinted yellows or pale yellows of youth through straw to golden yellow, gold, amber and possibly brown.

The following points refer particularly to red wines.

The eye or bowl shows the wine's principal hue. In general, but not always, deeper colours are those of wines from vineyards in latitudes closer to the equator, from good vintages and they presage more forceful impressions on the palate. Conversely, paler wines are likely to be more delicate in flavour and to come from further away from the equator or from cooler, less sunny vintages.

The rim is always watery at its very edge. This watery extremity widens as the wine ages and loses colour. The rim proper can be very informative in red wines. In broad terms a *narrow* rim indicates youth and wines with considerable extract, from small grapes with thick skins, the consequence of dry and sunny growing conditions. A *wider* rim is the result of less pigment and extract in the wine, suggesting a higher ratio of juice to skins during fermentation. This could be the result of a higher yield of grapes on the vine, thinner skins, or just less colour in the skins from a cooler, wetter growing season.

Rim *colour* always starts as a bluish-purple in newly made red wines, turning red and then brick coloured as the wine matures. How rapidly this change takes place depends on the grape variety and the character of the vintage. The degree of "browning", as it is often called, is more an indication of relative maturity (and readiness to drink) than of actual age in years. Browning will occur more rapidly in wines from certain grape varieties (Merlot, Grenache, and Nebbiolo for

example), in lighter vintages or in wines which have a relatively low acidity, often from sunny climes. And vice-versa.

Where does colour come from? *White wines:* The green tinge in some wines comes from chlorophyl left in their grape skins when the grapes are picked, for in cooler climates, even when the grapes are ripe the skins may not be completely translucent. It is not clear where the "yellow" of white wines comes from initially (a little may come from contact with air during pressing), but it gradually deepens as the wine absorbs oxygen during ageing. This is similar to an apple's flesh browning after it has been cut and left exposed to the air. Gewürztraminer, whose skin may be pinkish when ripe, often produces a wine that is a deeper yellow to start with and many sweet wines, particularly those from botrytized grapes, are also darker when young. Ageing in oak will produce a "yellower" white wine, and low acidity wines will also turn golden, and duller, more rapidly.

Red wines: Clearly the colour comes from the grape skins. It is due to a group of compounds called polyphenols, the most important of which are *anthocyanins* and *tannins*. The anthocyanins are purple and give a young wine its colour, but they precipitate fairly quickly (forming part of the wine's sediment) and the tannins, which are more red and yellow in hue, are then responsible for the browning effect in red wines as they mature.

(**Above**) *The colour of wine, red wine in particular, is never uniform, but deepest at the centre of the "eye", paling gradually towards the rim, and with numerous nuances in a fine, mature wine.*

Just how subtle its colours are can be seen by comparison with the flat, uniform appearance of the cochineal solution on the left.

THE SENSES: **SMELL**

THE IMPORTANCE OF SMELL

For the enjoyment of wine your sense of smell is the most important sense by a long way. A large proportion of what we call "taste" is in fact smell; a point that is easily demonstrated if you recall that to avoid tasting unpleasant medicine as a child you held your nose! And our sense of smell is a far more sensitive instrument than our palate. You need only taste with your nose held to appreciate the difference. Lingering over a really fine bouquet can be even more intoxicating than actually drinking the wine, with the considerable advantage that the source is not consumed.

Our sense of smell is rapidly tired. We have all had the experience of smelling a wonderful rose, for example, and of trying to prolong and intensify the sensation. Instead we find it diminishes and becomes less clear cut after a few seconds. This effect is called adaptation. However, if we stop smelling for a short while, the sense of smell recovers rapidly and we can soon go back to our rose, or whatever, and experience its full strength again.

How to "nose" a wine People vary as to which they find the most effective way to smell or "nose" a wine, and you may well find a combination works best. Try the following methods:

1. Short, sharp sniffs; best for a quick impression or

(Right) It is helpful to know how the sense of smell works; not only for how to go about sniffing, but also for understanding certain aspects of taste and how they are described. The organ of smell, the olfactory bulb, is located at the top of the nose. Molecules of "smell" must be in a vapour form (volatile) in order to be sensed, and they reach the olfactory bulb via two different routes: the nostrils and the passage connecting the nose to the throat, the rear nasal passage. This latter route contributes considerably to the taste and aftertaste of wine when we actually drink it. Simple wines have limited "aromatic" character; a wine with little bouquet will have little interest on palate or finish. Fine wines are complex and exciting precisely because they have an abundance of aromatic elements. This is what sustains their bouquet in the glass, their "flavour" on the palate and makes their aftertaste so lingering. Such wines can be described as "highly aromatic".

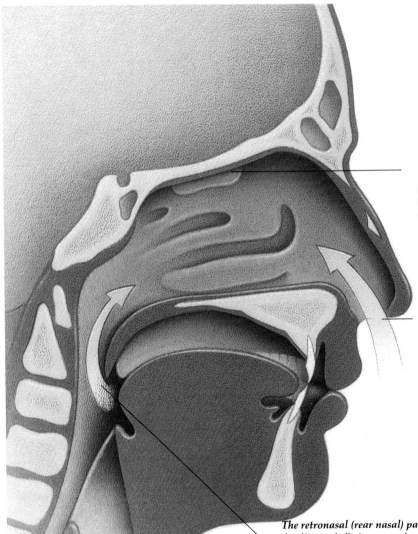

The olfactory bulb, centre of the sense of smell and a much more discriminating sense organ than the tongue.

The nostrils are the primary route to the olfactory bulb. They convey the aromas smelled in the glass. Wines that are impressive to smell in the glass will generally be very aromatic on the palate and on the finish as they have a lot to be perceived "retronasally".

The retronasal (rear nasal) passage is the secondary route to the olfactory bulb. It conveys the aromas volatized in the warmth of the mouth, accounting for most of what we interpret as taste, but which is in fact smell, aroma.

confirming a fault like excess sulphur dioxide (SO_2).

2. Deep, prolonged sniffing; strongest impressions early on; trying too hard is self defeating.

3. Short, gentle sniffing; often reveals smells that are fleeting, but fine.

4. Prolonged, gentle sniffing; I find this the best way to enjoy a really subtle bouquet. Barely inhaling can produce a very heady sensation, and your sense of smell is fatigued the least in this way.

Whichever you do, you need to concentrate hard to try and identify or describe smells as they appear, for you will find they reach a peak of intensity after four or five seconds and then diminish, at which point you need to rest for a few moments. Prolonged, insistent smelling is pointless for the reasons described above.

How to use your glass How you do this will have a telling effect on the extent to which you can smell all that a wine has to offer.

Swirling, or "taster's twitch". The following describes how to swirl. Once mastered, you will find yourself unconsciously swirling practically anything in a glass!

1. Unless you want to warm the contents of your glass by holding or cupping the bowl, always hold it by the bottom of the stem between thumb and one or two fingers. In any case this is the easiest way.

2. If you are right handed you will find it simpler to swirl anti-clockwise, and if you are left handed, try clockwise.

3. Swirl with the glass resting on the table until the movement comes easily, then it will present no problem up in the air.

4. With the glass still on the table, in a relaxed and gentle manner, begin to rotate the glass by the stem; you need hardly swivel the base more than a few millimetres from side to side, just enough to start the wine swirling. Once it has started, the gentlest and smallest of rotating movements will keep the wine circling up the sides of the glass. To agitate it a little more vigorously just requires a slightly bigger circle and a little more speed. The less you work, and the smaller your movements (from fingers, or wrist, at most) the easier it is. Off the table movement is exactly the same; in this case, where there is no surface to rest on, many tasters find that they can manipulate the glass best when holding it by the foot.

When smelling a wine, the temptation is always to give your glass a swirl and then sniff. Resist the temptation! If you only smell after swirling you are likely to miss a lot of the lighter, finer aromas which you

(**Left**) Holding a wine glass by the stem . . . the simplest way to hold one. This makes it easy to tilt for looking at colour, or to swirl.

(**Left**) Holding a wine glass by the foot . . . many people find they can manipulate the glass more comfortably held by its foot.

15

The three states in which to smell a wine

*1. When it is **still**: before swirling, and after it has been at rest again for a while. You can do this with the glass on the table, or picked up but not agitated. In this state you will smell some of the most delicate aromas, from those molecules which are the most volatile, and the most fleeting. These often show the "varietal character" of the grape most clearly, especially in a young wine.*

*2. **After swirling**: this increases the evaporating surface for the wine and encourages a greater number and wider variety of molecules to emerge. The odours in this state, whether finer or coarser, are generally more pronounced, often more penetrating. But they may also be less well defined, and in many cases the nose becomes "dumber", usually in a young wine. In simple wines there is not always much difference between "still" and "swirled". In wines with a really interesting bouquet there is often a progression of wonderful but tantalizingly fugitive scents which come and go for several seconds as the wine settles.*

*3. (**After shaking**) This is in brackets because you only need to do it if the wine is really "dumb" or closed", or if you suspect there is something unpleasant lurking and you want to confirm. Agitate the wine violently in the glass possibly with your hand over the top to prevent spilling.*

(Right) *Les Impitoyables: impressive for bouquet, though they emphasize alcohol. From left to right: Champagne, white, mature red (most attractive), young red (most versatile).*

will have just spent spinning out of the glass. Odour molecules emerge at different moments in time, depending on their volatility and on conditions such as temperature and whether the glass has been swirled or not. Thus there is often a sequence of smells to perceive, and this is why one needs to smell a wine in different states.

The three states in which to smell are shown left.

"Les Impitoyables": the merciless magnifiers. Earlier I sang the praises of the International Standards Organization glasses as the best all round tasting glasses. And I stick to that. But . . . for the nose alone, Les Impitoyables are the ultimate, if expensive, kit. Jacques Pascot, their French designer, glassmaker and wine buff, discovered that just a few millimetres difference in height affected the way in which the same glass yielded a wine's bouquet. This started five years of experiment which resulted in Les Impitoyables. The sheer size of these glasses (permitting a large volume of wine to be held) and their enormous surface for evaporation leading to a proportionately small opening make them very efficient, if rather unwieldy, bouquet gatherers. Pascot considers that if the ISO glasses are about 30 per cent efficient for a wine's bouquet, his are 80 per cent efficient! You may scoff, as I did, but just try them.

The source of wine odours The major source of the various smells in wine are the skin of the grape and just underneath it. From here come the characteristic "varietal aromas" that identify the best winemaking grape varieties: Cabernet Sauvignon's "blackcurrant" character, Sauvignon Blanc's "gooseberries", Merlot's

warm, buttery smell and so on. Soil is said to affect the aromas in the grape skin, and this doesn't seem too fanciful when you smell the earthiness in a Médoc or Graves, the minerally character in a German Mosel or in a Côte Rôtie from the northern Rhône. Fermentation itself gives wine its specific "vinous" odour, and yeasts are also considered to influence aromas during fermentation, although analyzing just how is not easy. Champagne certainly derives a "yeasty" smell from ageing on its yeast lees, and some cold fermented, early bottled white wines (from Australia in particular) are thought to get their grapefruity aroma from a selected yeast called R2. The most obvious odour characteristic given by fermentation or ageing in new oak is that of vanilla, commonly associated with red wines from Rioja and Chardonnay based wines from Burgundy and the New World. Finally there are the smells that develop with bottle age, the result of complex reactions between components in the wine in the absence of oxygen.

Describing smells is difficult and subjective at the best of times! Our vocabulary is limited; training, practice and consensus even more so. To say a wine smells of its grape variety (and many don't seem to) is a useful shorthand, but inadequate. Although a smell "suggested" is frequently a smell "found", it can be helpful to focus on a group of smell categories to see if any fit. The following is a list of useful categories with a few specific examples:

Floral: most commonly rose, violet, jasmine, acacia.
Fruity: blackcurrant, cherry, plum, peach, apricot, orange and lemon.
Spicy: pepper, clove, mint, truffle, liquorice, nutmeg, cinammon.
Animal: game, gamey, meaty, musk, damp fur/wet wool, cat's pee.
Vegetal: damp straw or hay, moss, undergrowth, mushroom, tea, greenery.
Mineral: chalky, volcanic, earthy.
Balsamic: anything resinous, pine, turpentine, briar; and in the sweeter sense, vanilla.
Chemical: fermentation odours, yeast, sulphur and its associated smells, ethyl acetate (nail varnish), mercaptan ("garlicy"), carbolic smell.
Empyreumatic: fire and heat associated smells, burnt or roasted characteristics; tar, toast, smoke, caramel.

Some of these may seem a bit arbitrary. They are. Where would you put "nutty", "honeyed", "leathery"?

(**Left**) *Nose and glass.* You may feel that where you put your nose in your glass in order to smell is second nature, but try these variations:

1. Nostrils close to the lower rim of the glass. Here, close to the surface of the liquid, you will smell the heavier, headier characteristics; I visualize them just lying along the bottom of the glass.

2. Nostrils close to the upper rim of the glass is better for the lighter, more delicate and subtle aspects.

3. Alternate nostrils. This seems quite irrational, but it sometimes helps to "get at" a bouquet if you tilt nose and glass so as to favour one and then the other nostril.

Not even the specialists can agree on the groupings. Regard them as pointers to help you locate smells if you are stuck for words. Some are very useful in a general way: floral, fruity, spicy and mineral; but I have never seen a nose described as "empyreumatic" (gap in the literature here!) One group which is not included above is not really of smells as such but of irritants, tactile sensations: acrid, sharp and pungent.

ASPECTS TO NOTE WHEN SMELLING

Cleanliness Every wine's nose should be clean; that is free from any unpleasant stink, mouldiness, acridity etc.

Intensity Most of the words you would use here are self explanatory: light, moderate, intense; and in a negative sense weak or limited. In a positive sense dumb, closed and undeveloped are used to describe a nose that doesn't smell of much at present, but which, usually after a thorough agitation, suggests there is something good to come. Penetrating describes a notable concentration and clarity of smells.

Grape variety Grape variety is the key to a wine's character and as such wines should smell clearly of their grape or grapes; at least when they are anything more than the most basic quality. Experience will show you what is typical and what is not for a given style. Reading books like this will suggest words to describe what is typical, but you should constantly search for your own vocabulary of "trigger words", to indentify characteristics which will pinpoint a grape for you. The comparative tastings suggested in the individual grape sections are the best way to practice this.

Non grape smells The most common of these to note is the influence of old or new wood in which the wine may have been aged. Other permanent or passing smells will be found in the list of defects.

Aroma and bouquet A moderately useful distinction. *Aroma* refers to the clear cut, fresh, vigorous fruit and spice characteristics originating from the grape. These are at their most obvious in young wines. An aromatic wine has these qualities in a marked way, a young Sauvignon Blanc from the Loire for example. *Bouquet* refers to the smells of mature wines, smells which develop as a result of ageing, particularly ageing in bottle. The character of the bouquet depends on the grape variety, quality of the wine, method of fermentation and ageing.* Its character is generally softer, rounder, mellower, more subtle and complex than its respective "aroma"; with scents that are sweeter, more vegetal, oilier or more nutty to name but a few of the characteristics.

* In Burgundy smells from the grape itself are known as primary aromas, those that result from fermentation and wood ageing are called secondary aromas, those from bottle age, tertiary aromas.

(**Right**) In Bordeaux, winetasters divide a wine's smells into aroma (smells from the grape) and bouquet (smells from fermentation, oak ageing and bottle age). The Burgundians, although they use the terms similarly, prefer to divide bouquet into secondary and tertiary aromas, with those from the grape being primary.

AROMA	BOUQUET	
BORDEAUX:		
🍇	FERMENTATION + OAK AGEING	BOTTLE AGE
BURGUNDY:		
🍇	FERMENTATION + OAK AGEING	BOTTLE AGE
PRIMARY AROMA	SECONDARY AROMA	TERTIARY AROMA

THE SENSES: TASTE AND TOUCH

WHERE TO LOOK FOR WHAT

Although smell does account for a large proportion of taste, there is no substitute for actually drinking! Indeed, a wine's aromas are exalted in the warm environment of the mouth, "on the palate" as wine-speak has it. One cannot concentrate on all the sensations in one's mouth at once. For this reason it is useful to know where you sense what, so that you can focus your attention deliberately and perceive more efficiently.

TASTES

Tastes are simpler than smells; we can isolate just four of them: sweet, acid, bitter and salty. They are sensed by taste buds sensitive to one particular taste. These buds are concentrated on different parts of the tongue. However, sweetness is no more exclusive to the tip of your tongue than acidity is to the sides; these traditionally sensitive areas are simply those where the individual tastes may be sensed particularly easily.

Tastes and your tongue Sweetness. Lick the tip of a finger, dip it in the sugar bowl and place it on the insensitive area in the middle of your tongue, avoiding the tip. Place your tongue against the roof of your mouth and slide it forward. You will taste the sugar very clearly as it moves over the back of your tongue. Taste a solution of water and sugar similarly, avoiding your tongue tip by placing it well forward under the glass. Once again the sweetness will be quite apparent all over the rear of your tongue. You can demonstrate the same thing to yourself with saltiness (fingertip and *very* little salt) and acidity (squeezed lemon juice diluted with water), by avoiding the traditionally sensitive areas. Bitterness, although you can get an inkling of it at your tongue tip, is more localized than the other tastes, and this time at the back of the tongue, seeming to stretch back into one's throat. Try a little cold, super concentrated coffee, and see how the bitter taste lingers there. This explains the comment on some wines that they are "bitter on the finish". Individual sensitivity to bitterness is the most variable of all the tastes, so don't be surprised if someone else finds a bitterness that you don't. Use these substances, in solid or soluble form, to demonstrate the traditionally sensitive areas as well.

Two super sensitive spots. There is a concentration of taste buds on either side of your tongue, right at the back, on the outer and upper edges, just next to the two rear molars. Dab them with a bit of sugar and you will feel a sensation of particular intensity.

The point is that the principal tastes are not limited to a particular area, and that when you taste wine you want to make sure you distribute it to as many parts of your palate as possible. Compare a sip of good wine which you simply *swallow immediately*, with a similar sip which you *work well round your palate*, into your cheeks and right to those sensitive spots at the back, before swallowing. Notice how much more you get from the wine, and how much more intensely it tastes?

TOUCH

In addition to the four basic tastes, the other categories of sensation on the palate relate to touch: astringency, body, temperature, carbon dioxide prickle and texture.

Astringency is the pulling, puckering sensation you feel when your gums, tongue and hard palate can no longer slide against each other comfortably; as though they had insufficient saliva. In wine this is usually due

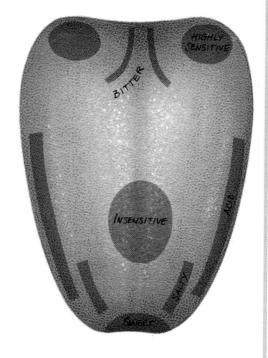

(**Left**) *The tongue is a much cruder organ for taste than the olfactory bulb for smell. The highlighted areas are those where the four primary tastes are sensed especially keenly but not exclusively:*
Sweetness: tip of the tongue
Saltiness: front, upper sides
Acidity: sides and upper sides
Bitterness: extreme rear, centre.
The sensitive zones are one reason for making sure you distribute the wine right round your mouth when tasting. Another is that there are two very sensitive areas in the rear sides of the tongue, which have a particularly high concentration of taste buds.

to tannin. Tannin modifies saliva and robs it of its slippery, lubricant qualities. Chew the skin of a grape, (the pips if you want an extreme example) and you will immediately feel what astringency is. High acidity can also have this effect.

Body is not a simple concept. It is a combination of intensity of flavour, density of texture and weight of alcohol. Body is sometimes said to be due to alcohol alone, and for a wine to have plenty of body certainly requires a fair level of alcohol; but without flavour and a consistency of texture to balance it, the feel of abundant alcohol is just hard and "hot". German Eisweins, on the other hand, are intense in flavour (very sweet) and have a palpable viscosity; but they lack body precisely because they are low in alcohol. Any impression of "wateriness" is a lack of body.

Temperature will be treated in detail later. It plays an important part in the way a wine feels. Depending on its degree it can modify, for better or for worse, the effects of alcohol, tannin, acidity and the refreshing aspect of lighter wines.

Carbon dioxide (CO_2), or "sparkle". When present in very small quantities, carbon dioxide is felt as a brief prickle just on the tip of the tongue.

Texture refers to the overall feel and consistency of a wine. It is a significant factor in quality. Useful comparisons can be made with fabrics and their weave: silky, velvety, satin-textured; loose knit or tight knit, for example; or with the feel and finish on other materials: glossy, polished, matt, granular, coarse or fine grained and so on. The analogies are a combination of the tactile and the visual.

(**Right and opposite**) *One can "feel" the texture of these fabrics and woods just by looking at them. The silk (top left) and sandalwood (opposite top) are both tightly woven, close textured and fine grained; whereas the wool (below left) and the cordia (opposite below) are loose knit, (literally for the wool), coarse textured and more "grainy" or rough in appearance and feel.*

Similar impressions of texture are experienced when working a wine round one's mouth, so that one can see why analogies with wood and materials, or adjectives such as glossy, polished, granular and so on can be so useful.

THE MECHANICS OF TASTING

We have already taken a detailed look at how to smell; this section is concerned with the practical details of "tasting" as opposed to "nosing".

How much wine to take At a tasting where expensive bottles are being shared you will only get about 35cl of each wine sample. This might seem rather little, but you will find you can get six to eight good tastes out of this; in fact you don't need a large mouthful. However, try too little wine and you will find you cannot get it to all your taste buds, it is rapidly diluted by saliva, and you tend only to taste the harsher aspects of the wine – acid, tannin and alcohol, not the fruit. If you take too much it is both difficult to manipulate in your mouth and awkward to

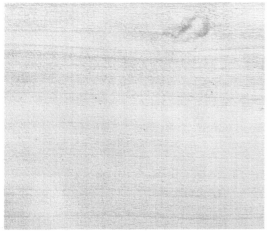

spit. A practical amount is a large teaspoon (5 to 6cl).

What to do with it Work the wine gently all around your palate using movements of your jaw, tongue and cheeks, making sure you get it to those taste buds right at the back. Swallow a little once or twice as you "chew" the wine, and draw a little air through it so as to help volatize the aromas. (The way to do this, so that you neither choke nor drip, is to keep the wine at the front of your mouth, place your front teeth against a slightly pouted lower lip, as though pronouncing "F", and then to suck as you would through a straw, rather than actually breathing in.) As you "work" the wine, concentrate on its different aspects one at a time so that you can note down its constitution (alcohol, acid, tannin etc) and its actual flavour. Swallow a little once more and then spit. Spit with conviction, otherwise you will dribble embarrassingly! Purse and pout your lips quite firmly, keep your jaws well apart and compress the wine out positively. If the wine trade is anything to go by there is a strong possibility that practice may *not* make your aim or trajectory perfect – keep trying!

How long to "chew" the wine Depends on how much you take and how good the wine is. I find I average between 15 and 20 seconds before spitting. If you keep the wine in your mouth much longer you will probably find it begins to become watery from dilution with saliva, or else you are gradually swallowing it all!

Finish and aftertaste Having spat, breathe out through your nose and mouth and see how long the sensations of taste and aroma persist. I am frequently asked what the distinction is between *finish*, *aftertaste* and *length*. The aftertaste is part of the finish, and length qualifies them both. When describing the taste of a wine in detail, its progress on the palate is described in terms of an "attack" followed by a "development" or "evolution", followed in turn by the finish. The finish comprises all the sensations you experience as and after you swallow for the last time or spit the wine out; it involves sensations of texture as well as taste and aroma. To take extremes: a wine may feel unpleasantly hard or acid or tannic as you swallow it, or soft, supple and pleasing. If the harder, coarser sensations persist, they may well spoil or dominate the aftertaste; if the finish is too soft then the aftertaste may lack support, feel short and limp.

Aftertaste refers just to the sensations of taste and aroma (not texture) which persist after swallowing, "on the finish" that is. Length describes how long all the sensations of the finish last for.

A SUMMARY OF TASTING TECHNIQUES

SIGHT

Actions
1. With the glass vertical, view the wine from directly above.
2. With the glass tilted, view the wine at an angle against a white background.
3. Having swirled the wine, look horizontally across the glass at eye level.

What to look at and record:

Brilliance of the wine's surface, clarity and depth of colour, any CO_2.

SMELL

Actions
4. Before swirling, smell the wine still.
5. Swirl the wine, then smell it immediately, continuing to sniff as it settles. To get the most out of the glass vary the relationship of nose to glass.
6. Agitate violently, possibly covering the rim of the glass with your hand.

What to look for and record:

Finer varietal qualities, finesse, persistence of aroma/bouquet.

TASTE

Actions
7. Take a sip, about the size of a large teaspoonful.
8. Distribute the wine all round the palate; swallow a little, aerate, work the wine gently and swallow a little more.
9. Spit, breathe out through nose and palate, smack lips and palate for final savour.

What to look for and record:

Initial "attack": whether it is soft or firm and how soon the harsher sensations of acid and/or tannin appear, any CO_2 prickle.

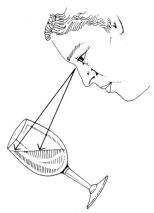

Principal hue in the "eye" of the wine, width and hue of the "rim", colour nuance.

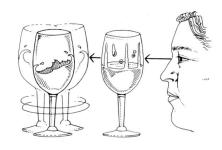

Viscosity, "legs" or "arches" as a possible indicator of weight.

Differences from the "still' state, heavier, more intense smells, a progression of scents as the wine settles.

To waken a "dumb" nose, or confirm a suspected fault.

Development: flavours proper, aromatic character; intensity and variety and how well these are sustained; quality of texture.

Finish: final impressions of texture, length of aftertaste, and the balance of "tastes" and "aromas" in the aftertaste.

RECORDING IMPRESSIONS: DESCRIBING STYLE

Where does one start when trying to describe a wine's taste? If you have little experience in making notes it is easier to begin by concentrating on one aspect at a time, and to distinguish description from appraisal to start with. In this way, by comparing wines with a marked contrast, you will develop your awareness of the different aspects of wine and of the vocabulary used to describe them.

NOTING THE BASIC FACTS

Remember the aim here is to *describe*, not to judge. In other words "what it's like" as distinct from "whether I like it" or "how good it is". This is akin to describing a person's build and colour: fat or thin, tall or short, white or black, irrespective of their personality ... nice or nasty. In the case of a wine this is its *constitution* or *structure*: light or heavy, soft or acidic, smooth or tannic and so on, a *quantitative summary* rather than a qualitative one. White wines have a simpler structure than reds (because they have no tannin) and are therefore easier to start with. Comparing just two

bottles is easiest, but three or four (or more if palate and purse can stand it) will be more instructive, and a group sharing costs and impressions makes the whole exercise more fruitful as well as more economical. That said, you will probably find six wines is more than enough to take a detailed "look" at initially.

PROCEDURE

Most of the suggested wines should be readily available from good wine merchants or supermarkets. They have been selected so as to demonstrate differ-

> 1. Taste the samples fairly quickly, distributing the wine well round your palate, but concentrating on the main characteristic you are comparing.
>
> 2. Write down one or two adjectives to describe this for each wine. You may find it easier to put the wines in order of increasing acidity, alcohol and so on, as listed, before choosing your comparative descriptions.
>
> 3. Taste from left to right first, then in reverse order to confirm your first impressions.
>
> 4. If you get confused stop and rest. Have a rinse with water and eat a dry biscuit before starting again.

(Right) *Comparing components: acidity* For each category of wine here (dry white, red, sweet white and medium sweet white) there are three broad acidity groups, from left to right: low acid, medium acid and high acid. A comparison, within the category, of any of the wines from different groups should help your perception of acidity. One each from the "low" and "high" group, would make the best contrast. The upper sides of your tongue are where to look for acidity.

The first wine you taste often seems more acid than it really is. This is because your palate is fresh, and it is worth going back after you have tasted a few more wines. Number one invariably tastes softer then!

	low acidity	in between	high acidity
DRY WHITE	Table white Mâcon Blanc White Burgundy (1983) (Côte de Beaune)	Chablis (not Grand Cru) South Tyrol Chardonnay White Burgundy (1985) (Côte de Beaune)	Sancerre Alsace Riesling White Burgundy (1984/86) (Côte de Beaune)
RED	1982 Claret (lesser St Emilion esp.) Australian Shiraz South African Pinotage	1984 Claret Chianti Beaujolais Villages 1984 Red Burgundy	Reds from the Loire or Tasmania Barbera
SWEET WHITE	Generic Sauternes	Good quality Barsac or Sauternes	Coteaux du Layon or Bonnezeaux from the Loire
MEDIUM SWEET WHITE	Rheinhessen Spätlese Rheinpfalz Spätlese	Rheingau Spätlese (same vintage)	Mosel Spätlese (same vintage)

For any of these you could add cream of tartar by "pinches" or lemon juice by drops to a glass of wine to increase acidity and see the effect this has.

ences of one aspect in particular (acidity, alcohol, tannin etc) but you will want to compare appearance, nose and other characteristics as well, although the distinctions may not be quite so clear.

Acidity Concentrate on the upper sides of your tongue. Notice how it "shapes" and "defines" the wine, gives an attractive life and zip to the flavour, keeps the taste going on the finish – or not!

The bold words are undesirable extremes and would usually be considered terms of criticism. The list is in order of increasing acidity from absence to excess. As with most wine terms these are relative, not absolute; common sense and the range you are tasting will tell you what is appropriate:

flat, flabby, shapeless – soft, fresh, lively, crisp, mouthwatering, vigorous, firm, hard – **sharp, green, tart, acid** . . . All of which you can qualify with quite, fairly, very etc. Any selection from the different groups should give you good examples of varying acidity.

Alcohol Alcohol is "felt" rather than "tasted", although at high levels it does increase the impression of sweetness. It is mainly sensed as "weight" or presence on the whole palate, allied to a certain warmth. You can use a bottle of Vodka to give you a good idea of the effect of different degrees of alcohol by preparing the following solutions: (use equal measures).

	Vodka (37° – 40°)	+	Water	Approx. total degrees alcohol
a)	1	+	1	19°
b)	1	+	2	12.5°
c)	1	+	3	9.5°
d)	1	+	4	7.5°
e)	1	+	5	6.5°

And to see what too much alcohol does to a wine, use a dry white of about 11°/12°, and to 1 measure of solution "a" (19°) add 1 measure of wine. This will bring your wine up to 15° – 16°. Notice how more alcohol not only makes the wine "heavier" and more mouthfilling, but also "hotter" and "harder", possibly more bitter as well. (This experiment will inevitably dilute the flavour a bit.)

It is difficult to separate the impression of alcohol alone from that of texture and depth of flavour, and some terms refer to more than just alcohol. The list is in order of increasing "weight".

watery, weak, meagre – light-, medium-, full-bodied, warm, ample, generous, heady – **heavy, alcoholic, hot.**

	low alcohol	in between	high alcohol
DRY WHITE	"Low alcohol" or "Alcohol Free" wine, Vinho Verde	Chablis (plain) Bulgarian Chardonnay	Chablis Grand Cru White Hermitage Dry Sherry
SWEET WHITE	German Auslese Asti Spumante	Sauternes	Muscat de Beaumes de Venise Samos Muscat
RED	Rosé d'Anjou Generic Bordeaux	Beaujolais Villages Generic St Emilion	Tavel (red or rosé) Châteauneuf du Pape

(Left) *Comparing components: alcohol For each category of wine here (dry white, sweet white and red) there are three broad alcohol groups, from left to right: low alcohol, medium alcohol and high alcohol. A comparison, within the category, of any of the wines from different groups should help your perception of alcohol. Notice how alcohol is perceived not just as an impression of "weight" and "warmth", but how it also spreads and prolongs the flavour sensations on your palate. The comparison with a low alcohol or alcohol-free wine is a particularly instructive one.*

It is always worth going back and tasting in reverse order. This often puts the wines in a new perspective, or reveals aspects that you hadn't noticed the first time round.

Tannin More of a texture than a taste, although when it is abundant it can have a bitter flavour; and from particularly ripe grapes it often yields a spicy, aromatic character too. "Chew" the wine well and look for the dry, "furry", puckering sensation on the surfaces of your mouth; on the roof, and between gums and cheeks especially. Easy to confuse with acidity (which can have a similar "drying" effect); if you are in doubt, focus on the upper sides of your tongue to check whether it is acidity or not.

Because tannin is perceived primarily as texture there are more words to describe its *quality* than its *quantity*. Quantity: lightly tannic, moderately tannic, very tannic. Quality: fine (-grained), soft, supple, dry, rich, firm, chewy, hard, **tough, rough, coarse, vegetal, stemmy, bitter, astringent.**

(**Right**) *Comparing components: tannin Here are three groups of red wine with, from left to right, low tannin, medium tannin and high tannin. A comparison between any wine from the "low" group and any from the "high" group will illustrate the astringent nature of tannin very clearly. Tannin is very difficult to quantify and it is the quality of its texture that is important. Fineness of tannin texture is one of the key elements that distinguishes a top quality red wine from one that is merely good, and what makes a First Growth claret or a Grand Cru burgundy, for example, deserving of that status. Work the wine well round your mouth and try to assess both quantity and quality.*

(**Right**) *La Brezza cellar in Barolo. Tasting any more than a few Barolos is very demanding on one's palate, not to mention one's concentration, because of the rapid build up of tannin in the mouth. Here a Barolo producer takes time off to concentrate on something very different, a Vin Jaune of Jean Bourdy's.*

low tannin	in-between	high tannin
Valpolicella	Rioja	Barolo
Bulgarian Merlot	Australian Cabernet/Shiraz	Barbaresco
South African Cabernet	Crozes-Hermitage	1975/1986 Claret
1982 Burgundy	St Emilion	Most St-Estephe
Beaujolais Nouveau		Many Californian Cabernets

Flavour If wines tasted of acid, alcohol and tannin alone, I would not be writing a book about them and you certainly wouldn't want to read it. These are just the bare bones which support flavour; it is wine's infinite variety of flavours which distinguishes it from other beverages and which makes us want to discuss and communicate its pleasures in a way which would seem bizarre with the majority of drinks. The most obvious component of flavour is its "fruit" characteristic, and in simple wines the main appeal is a "fruity" one. Flavour must balance the impressions of alcohol, acid and (in reds) tannin; and as such it is the final part of the wine's basic make-up that you need to note. How *much* flavour, for all wines, and how *sweet or dry* for white wines, are essential to note.

Flavour of what? Most people relate wine's actual flavour (as opposed to its texture, balance and development) to those of *fruits*, for example: blackcurrants, plums, damsons, mulberries, cherries; oranges, tangerines, lemons, grapefruit; peaches, pears, apples, lychees and so on; to *spices*: vanilla, clove, cinammon, nutmeg, pepper; to *mineral impressions* such as earthiness, chalk, tar, oil, gravel, stones etc; and to a host of other *common flavours* such as bread, yeast, honey, toast, caramel, butter, cream, mint, various nuts, chocolate – the list is infinite and often fanciful.

Dry/Sweet Dry, in relation to wine, means, an absence of sweetness; and while it may be difficult to decide *how* sweet, we all know what the sensation is. You will want to note the amount of flavour in all the wines whose constitution you are describing:
empty, lacking in flavour, dilute – light, moderately or abundantly flavoured, fruity, flavoursome, rich intense, concentrated. (Dry to sweet) bone-dry, dry, off-dry, medium-dry; slightly sweet, medium-sweet, sweet, intensely sweet.

EXPANDING YOUR NOTES
If you have been concentrating on comparing and describing the individual acid, alcohol, tannin and flavour aspects of various wines, you will most likely have ended up with a rather disjointed collection of adjectives. At this stage it is worth moulding them into a brief phrase summarizing the wine's constitution. For example, a Mâcon Blanc for which you might have noted the following:

> Acidity: soft
> Alcohol: full-bodied
> Flavour: moderately fruity, dry

could be summarized as: *A full bodied wine; soft, dry and moderately fruity.* Or: *A soft, dry, full bodied and moderately fruity wine.* Similarly, a Barolo noted as:

> Alcohol: generous
> Acidity: firm
> Tannin: astringent
> Flavour: abundant

might be summarized as: *A generous wine with astringent tannin and firm acidity, but also abundant flavour.* Or: *Abundantly flavoured wine; generous, firm and astringent.* In this latter, shorter phrase, "firm" is understood as a word referring to acidity, "astringent" as one describing tannin; for these are their usual contexts in wine description. The first phrase also differs in a more significant way; the word "but" makes an implicit comment about balance: the wine has a lot of alcohol, tannin and acidity *but* it has enough flavour to balance these otherwise harsh elements. You will soon find you want to make implicit or explicit comments on balance when describing the wine's constitution. For example, a generic Sauternes noted as: *soft, heavy, sweet* (the three terms belonging respectively to acidity, alcohol and flavour groups) could be summarized to include a balance comment as: *A sweet and heavy wine with inadequate supporting acidity.* Or, more tersely: *Sweet and heavy, but too soft.*

A phrase summarizing and relating the elements thus will give you a clearer image of the wine as well as making your notes easier to read when you or others return to them (the same goes for notes on appearance, colour and smell). It is also worth getting into the habit of always noting elements in the same order so that you are unlikely to miss anything important when confronted with a large number or variety of wines.

On the subject of habit and elements to note, always make sure you note the *wine's identity* (full name, vintage, producer or shipper) and the *date of the tasting note*. These are *essential* if the information is to be of any use later. Optional information includes where and with whom, price and possibly food, (if you are drinking the wine as opposed to just tasting it). Years later I find I am always glad to have noted "where and with whom", for wines can be as evocative of people, place and occasion as scents and music. Great wines will recall the occasion without any reminder, lesser wines need a prompt, so the moment of time taken to record that prompt will be well rewarded.

RECORDING IMPRESSIONS:
EVALUATING QUALITY

HOW "GOOD" THE WINE TASTES

In the last section we looked at the more objective facts about a wine and briefly considered balance. Here I want to consider how one decides whether a wine is just "sound" or alternatively something special, how one distinguishes the ordinary from the fine.

Absence of faults A wine without faults is called *clean*. The majority of faults are chemical or biological in origin and cause unpleasant smells, tastes or textures. A wine with faults is called *dirty* or *out of condition*. Unless a fault is thought to be a temporary one the wine is unlikely to make the good quality ratings.

Balance Balance implies neither excess nor deficit of any component. There must be sufficient but not too much: sufficient acidity to preserve the wine, to give it definition on the palate and, if it is sweet, to stop it from being cloying; sufficient alcohol and fruit to balance the tannin in a red wine; sufficient tannin in the first place to provide colour, flavour, aroma and so on. Too much alcohol, acid, tannin, or even sugar are going to be unpleasant by definition. Think of what makes a good apple (crisp and juicy), or a bad one (soft and cottonwoolly); a good tomato (plenty of flavour and acidity), or a poor one (overripe and watery, lacking flavour and acid); or consider how you add milk and sugar to tea or coffee, salt and pepper to what you cook. These are all considerations relating to the "balance" of tastes and textures. The principles are the same for wines, both in terms of balancing the basic elements, and in that there is no *one* ideal style. What constitutes good balance varies from region to region and grape to grape, just as it does between oranges and pears, tomatoes and peas.

Perfectly balanced wines have an unmistakably "perfect" feel about them, but exactly what is meant by "well balanced" varies considerably. Just as the balance within a string quartet is very different from that within a symphony orchestra, so wines with component parts of very different proportions can be well balanced. A dry white from the Loire will have a higher proportion of acidity, and thus a more tart flavour, than a dry wine from the Mediterranean coast, but they can both be perfectly balanced, just

different in style. There is no one perfect set of proportions, balance relates to origin and any balance judgements must take this into account.

Young wines are sometimes said to be "unbalanced" or "not yet in balance", implying that they will acquire balance as they mature. I feel it makes more sense, if you think the requisite proportions for the style are there, to say instead that the wine is *balanced but not yet harmonious*. That is, you may be able to perceive the acid, alcohol, tannin and fruit as "separate" on the palate, but you feel the equilibrium is appropriate. Wines which are poorly balanced when young rarely become balanced with age, particularly where the problem is one of deficit. Wines *lose* fruit, tannin and acid, literally, as they age, but they cannot *gain*

(**Right and opposite**) *These two bottles contain dry white wines of very different styles because they come from different climates and are made from different grapes. The Savennières (left) comes from a cool climate, the Loire region in France, and it has both more acidity and less alcohol than the white Hermitage (right), which is high in alcohol and relatively low in acidity. Though they taste quite different they are both well balanced examples of their type. It would not make sense to criticise the Savennières for being rather firm and the Hermitage for being soft. That is their nature. Whether you like them is an entirely different matter.*

Texture As I have already implied, fine texture is very much a quality attribute, but one which is often difficult to separate from impressions of flavour and development. Coarse textures are not only inherently unpleasant but make any refinement of flavour difficult to perceive. Such textures are **harsh, hard, angular, coarse, rough**, in contrast to quality ones which are **smooth, round, supple, rich, silky, velvety, glossy** and so on.

Length of finish Put simply, the longer pleasant sensations of flavour and aroma persist noticeably after you have swallowed, the better the wine is – the more value you are getting for your money. Simpler wines tend to have an aftertaste which consists mainly of fruit or flavour, as opposed to aroma. These are sensations which you can taste right down the back of your tongue and into your throat. An aromatic aftertaste, found mainly in finer wines, is smelled primarily. It is a sensation that you might visualize as a fine mist of aromas which suffuses the whole oral cavity; an echo, a resonance of what has gone before. It is perceived by the sense of smell (via the rear nasal passage) as you breathe out. As such it often mirrors what your nose smells from the glass. To distinguish between fruit or flavour and aroma on the aftertaste, hold your nose as you swallow and you will only "taste" fruit and flavour. Let your nose go and you will sense/smell "aroma".

Great wines will combine both of these sensations, although one may continue for longer than the other. The aftertaste, whether flavour or aroma, can be qualified in terms of its intensity (light or pronounced) as well as its length. Lesser wines should have a distinct finish at least, but one cannot expect much length from them, "short but distinct" would not be unduly critical in this case. A "hollow" wine, however, has no finish whatsoever. Its flavour seems to disappear almost as soon as you have sipped it, certainly before you have finished swallowing. It is one of the most vividly descriptive, critical wine terms.

> The phrase "long on the palate" is often used to indicate a long *aftertaste*, but to avoid confusion with a long *development* on the palate I should distinguish between the two. They are *not* the same, although a wine which has a long development is likely to have a long aftertaste or "finish" as well.

Completeness A wine which satisfies the eye, nose, palate and which has a good finish is complete. If any of these categories are unsatisfactory, the wine disappoints to that extent and its quality is diminished.

what was not there in the first place. Good wines are well balanced from birth.

Intensity and concentration versus delicacy and finesse It is easy to be impressed by lots of flavour and forceful wines; they are the ones that always do well in comparative blind tastings. For wines that are more delicate and less concentrated, focussing on their development to the palate – a concept fully explored over the page – will give you an independent guide to their quality, and will often reveal subtleties that are easily overlooked when you are just concentrating on the "amount" of flavour. Conversely, examining the development of a wine that initially impresses with its abundance of flavour may reveal that it has little to offer beyond this.

(**Right and opposite**) *The types of wines illustrated and listed under the A, B and C columns would provide good comparisons to illustrate the notion of "development on the palate", an element of quality which is independent of the wine's style. It is a useful universal quality criterion which you can apply to any type of wine.*

The wines in the nearest picture are Riesling wines, and those listed below are all dry or sweet white wines. Those in the right hand picture are Cabernet or Cabernet based wines, and those listed below are all red wines.

Both pictures include a fourth bottle in column C, the fine wine column. They are examples of very expensive *wines which it would be deliciously instructive to include in your line up, but which aren't necessary to illustrate the point.*

NB: For a given region try to compare the **same vintage**, and in Burgundy or Alsace the **same producers'** wines. See part 2 for recommended producers.

Development on the palate* Cleanliness, balance and length are normally cited as three elements of quality, and so they are. Less attention is paid to the way in which a wine develops on the palate, not only the variety of individual flavours, but the progression of sensations and length of time their intensity and variety is sustained whilst the wine remains in the mouth. It is certainly difficult to describe, but it is a key quality factor and always worth conscious attention. "Complexity" and "layers of flavours" are descriptions which hint at the sensation, but neither involves the important sense of *evolution over a period.*

The best way to discover this is to take three wines of the same type, all good, but of significantly different quality. There is no substitute for at least one expensive bottle, and the demonstration is worth it.

In crude terms "development on the palate" is a question of *how much* you feel happening on the palate as you keep and gently work the wine in your mouth, and for *how long* your palate continues to feel stimulated, actively massaged almost, so that you want to go on savouring the wine before swallowing.

The simple wine (A) As soon as you sip it this wine will have an attractive but one dimensional fruit flavour, and there will be little sense of definition to the texture. Its appeal on the palate will be brief; keeping it there will not yield any additional flavours, nor any feeling of sustained stimulation of your taste buds. In other words its pleasure is all on the attack, it doesn't "evolve" or "develop" much, it is as though the liquid rapidly becomes inert, lifeless. In this case the wines development on the palate is **short**. It may be very attractive, but it is of **limited** interest, basic and straightforward.

The middle quality wine (B) This will taste of several flavours which will seem to increase in depth for a while as you retain and work the wine around your palate; it will also feel more **textured** and better **defined**. You will have a positive impression of variety and of active stimulation as the wine "develops" for several seconds. The liquid will appear to remain alive and **vibrant** for a measureable span so that you want to keep it in your mouth and savour it for some time. After a while though, the intensity of sensation will drop, you will feel it is no longer "active", and it is then time to swallow and enjoy the

* This has nothing whatsoever to do with a wine's "development" in the sense of how mature or immature it is, whether it is, or is not, ready to drink.

A
Dry Riesling
Co-operative Riesling
Sweet Semillon
Generic Sauternes/Barsac
Chardonnay
Inexpensive Australian
Inexpensive Californian
Puligny Montrachet

B
Dry Riesling
Riesling Reserve (Trimbach)
Sweet Semillon
Ch.Doisy Daene (Barsac)
Chardonnay
Rosemount Reserve
Mondavi Chardonnay
Puligny Montrachet 1er Cru

aftertaste. Here there has been a progression of sensations, a period during which intensity and variety have been sustained; the wine's development on the palate has been **positive** and of **medium length.** This wine has more interest and personality, more to relish … its quality is on a higher level.

The fine wine (C) will not only have an **abundance** and **concentration** of flavours, but these will come and go with a particular **clarity**. The texture will have a notable "fineness", a sense of **weave**, sug-

C	A	B	C
Dry Riesling	**Cabernets**	**Cabernets**	**Cabernets**
Riesl.Fred.Emile (Trimbach)	Basic Australian Cab.S.	Orlando "St Henri" Cab.S.	Leconfield Coonawarra Cab.S.
Sweet Semillon	Basic Californian Cab.S.	Stags Leap Napa Valley Cab.S.	Carmenet or Cl.du Bois "Marlstone"
Ch.Climens or Ch.d'Yquem	**Syrah**	**Syrah**	**Syrah**
Chardonnay	Crozes-Hermitage (Jaboulet)	Crozes-Herm. "Thalabert" (Jab)	Hermitage "La Chapelle"(Jab)
Lake's Folly or Mount Mary	Penfolds Bin 28 Shiraz	Cape Mentelle Shiraz	Magill Estate or Grange Hermitage
Mondavi Chard. "Reserve"	**Pinot Noir**	**Pinot Noir**	**Pinot Noir**
Chevalier or Bâtard-Montrachet	Morey St Denis	Morey St Denis 1er Cru	Clos St Denis or Cl.de La Roche

gesting a tightly woven or opulent fabric, a glossy or polished surface. Above all the wine's development to the palate will be distinct and prolonged: a layering, unfurling succession of sensations whose intensity and vitality are sustained for tens of seconds and more with no impression of abating. Whatever their style, from delicate to potent, such wines seem to have an inner charge of energy, a drive and vibrancy on the palate that makes you gasp with pleasure and admiration. These are wines whose development can be described as **long, prolonged, sustained**; in a style that may vary from subtle and beguiling, through even, elegant, graceful or harmonious, to vital, forceful, vigorous and so on.

If great wines are usually unmistakably great, this concept of temporal "development on the palate" is that much more useful as a means of quality discrimination amongst the less exalted; at whose lowest extremity are wines whose development may be described as plain, empty, lacking, dull, blunt.

(**Below**) *An analysis of three examples of tasting notes made about the same wine as that illustrated opposite:*
EXAMPLE 1
Medium colour/Light nose, good finish/Good flavour and balance/Tannin and acid. *Two "goods" suggest it's attractive. The rest is too vague. All reds have "tannin and acid" – how much of each? "Flavour" – of what? "Good balance" – for what type of wine? What is the quality level? Is it ready? Overall confused order.*
EXAMPLE 2
Garnet red/Nice if rather lean nose/Moderately full, mature flavour, still with some tannin and acid . . . medium length finish/Quite good, ready and will keep. *A better indication of quality and maturity, but still little idea of the actual flavours and quality level. "Quite good" – for what? Bulgarian Cabernet or classed growth Bordeaux? Could be almost any red grape.*
EXAMPLE 3
Mature garnet/Light, earthy Cabernet nose/Well balanced medium bodied wine, fresh and lightly tannic/ Straightforward, flavoury, earthy Medoc, medium length. Good of type and 78 vintage. Mature, will keep if not improve much. *A more precise and useful note than the 2nd example; and, while still economical in length, it does attempt to describe the characteristics of smell and flavour, the wine's quality level and how good it is for its type and year. Most useful, detailed notes will be about this length.*

RECORDING IMPRESSIONS:
WIDER APPRAISAL

So far we have looked at describing the basic facts about wines and then evaluating their taste qualities. But there are other questions you may want to ask, questions which will require differing kinds of answer. The reply to *What is it like?* (relatively objective), will not be the same as that to *Do you like it?* (entirely subjective), or *Is it value for money?* (fairly subjective; it depends on the competition at that level, and on how deep your pocket is for luxuries). Similarly, conflicting responses may be involved in replies to the questions *Is it good wine?* and *Is it good of its kind?* (Yes, it's well made, well balanced and attractive to taste – No, it's not what I consider typical). Whether you want to address all these questions or not, having the different issues clearly distinguished in your mind makes for more efficient and more accurate tasting, and a good tasting note will not confuse them.

"Is it good of its kind?" requires considerable tasting experience to be able to answer confidently. It is an important one to ask however, for we cannot sample every bottle before purchase; instead we buy on the basis of the label and what it leads us to expect. The trade in wine, and its enjoyment, would be impossible without a reasonable degree of consistency behind the label. Not only is our enjoyment of wine enhanced to some extent by knowing what to expect, but our judgement is rightly based on how the wine lives up to those preconceptions of style, quality and flavour.

Developing a clear idea of styles also means we can judge different wines appropriately, relating what is in the bottle to standards of quality, flavour and balance that have become accepted for a particular brand, grape variety or region. To say that a wine is a good or bad example of its kind on any other basis makes no sense.

SCORING

A figure by itself is virtually meaningless. If you do use figures to assess a wine, an overall figure is generally more reliable than one which is a sum of scores for individual parts. A single fault can mar a wine out of all proportion to its "size", so that however technically correct the rest of the wine seems you still won't want to drink it! No "add up" system that I know can take this into account, whereas it certainly can produce some weirdly misleading results. After all, it only takes one out of tune musician to ruin the sound of the rest who are playing perfectly in tune. Any scoring needs to be explicitly or implicitly related to a category of wine. A perfect Beaujolais should score 10/10 or 20/20, so should a perfect Grand Cru Burgundy, but the identical figure clearly has a different significance in each case.

As an additional means of situating a wine in relation to its peers or to wines at the same tasting, a figure can be a useful *supplement* to a note. But if figures become your principal means of assessment you will find yourself paying scant attention to the wine's various facets in the first place, and in six months or six years time you will have no idea what it was really like. On the basis of "I don't know what I think until I see what I write", searching for the right words not only helps you remember a wine but it helps you discover it in the first place.

Just as figures are an easy way out of "noting" a wine when we taste, pen in hand, so most of us have also been guilty of lazily reading wine writers' scores and not their notes, or only the notes of the high fliers. Wine merchants in America mutter bitterly that if a wine in Robert Parker's *Wine Advocate* scores above 90 they can't *acquire* it to sell, whereas if it scores below 90 they can't *sell* it! We are probably the poorer for that in more senses than one.

HOW MUCH TO WRITE?
Simple wines – simple notes; great wines – well, you could write simple notes on those too, but you will probably be tempted to write more. What matters is what you want that note to tell you in future. If all you want to know is whether the wine is good value or not your note might just consist of "great" or "lousy". If you want it to recall a great wine on a memorable occasion it may become an extended piece of purple prose. It is probably more helpful to make your notes too long rather than too short to start with, and to try and extend your active vocabulary (you can always prune later), but for a hardened taster economy pays.

WHAT TO WRITE
Examples of good and poor notes on a good Cru Bourgeois claret appear, with comment and analysis, in the margin of this page and in the fully annotated illustration opposite.

A sample tasting sheet with the anatomy of a thorough tasting note

CHÂTEAU
La Tour de By
1978
CRU BOURGEOIS DU MÉDOC

MÉDOC
APPELLATION MÉDOC CONTROLÉE
Bouteille — № 239246
Ste VITICOLE DU MEDOC "CHATEAU LA TOUR DE BY" 33340 BÉGADAN
12% vol   PRODUCE OF FRANCE   75cl

WHERE TASTED	DATE
BORDEAUX	21-5-85
VINTAGE	**WINE**
1978	Ch. La Tour de By Cru Bourgeois, Médoc

Name and any other appropriate details

APPEARANCE
Mature, brick rimmed garnet.

Colour and evidence of maturity

NOSE
Distinctive, earthy Cabernet nose with a touch of raw blackcurrant and no new oak evident.

Grape variety and how expressed

Any "non-grape" smells

PALATE
①Fresh, medium bodied, lightly tannic wine ② with a straightforward but nicely sustained ③ dry, earthy Cabernet flavour ④ and modest, faintly aromatic aftertaste of medium length.

(1) Basic constituents (Acid, alcohol, tannin)
(2) Quality as shown by development on the palate

(3) Actual flavours and/or aromas
(4) Length and quality of aftertaste or finish

ASSESSMENT
Very nicely balanced lesser Médoc, stressing fruit rather than finesse or complexity, but without any coarseness. A good example of Cru Bourgeois, and of the elegant, medium-weight 1978 vintage. Ready, will keep and soften, if not improve much.

How good is it for its type and vintage? Experience and comparative tastings will enable you to make such judgements with confidence

Readiness to drink, future prospects

SCORE

Optional!

Design your own small tasting sheets and have your local printer print them. One wine per sheet (otherwise you cannot index or file them properly) so there is no point in printing both sides. This makes for a very flexible storage system.

The last note is longer, yes! but it has plenty of evocative detail which reflects attentive tasting and care in the choice of words to describe character and quality. It provides a more thorough assessment which situates the wine's performance in relation to its status and vintage; i.e. how good is it for what it claims to be? (Cru Bourgeois quality from a good vintage). In other words, does it live up to its label? This length of note needs time, but it is increasingly worthwhile, the finer the wine.

TASTING EQUIPMENT

Glasses: one per person for a standing tasting (they can always be rinsed); as many as appropriate or practical for seated tastings.

Spittoons: an individual or shared beaker is desirable for seated tasters. For stand up tastings any large container such as a domestic bucket or washing-up bowl will do. Splashes are best avoided by a deep receptacle or by putting sawdust, woodshavings, cat (continued on p.35)

PRACTICALITIES

No amount of reading and advice can make up for personal experience in discovering just what suits your own particular environment. These are a few guidelines for tastings, formal or informal.

LOCATION

Stand up tastings The guiding principle is to have room to pour, room to move, room to write and room to spit without getting in other people's way. If you can achieve that your layout will be perfect! Too many wines or people in too little space is a recipe for frustration and wet disaster.

Sit down tastings Here you need to allow for several glasses (four to eight usually), an A4 size tasting sheet, a spittoon (shared or individual), space for biscuits on plates and water in bottles or jugs. Unless you have abundant table space, folding bridge tables are very practical. Four to one of these is a bit of a squeeze but possible, two to a table is positively extravagant.

Lighting Indirect daylight is ideal but usually impractical. Standard bulbs are better than fluorescent strips for artificial lighting. Both tend to "dull" the appearance, somewhat, and both make red wines look browner and older. A plain white background is easy to provide for sit down tastings: white tablecloths,

napkins, kitchen rolls are all suitable. For regular tastings it is worth purchasing white *plastic* sheeting which can be wiped clean each time. For stand up tastings a suitably lit white background should be accessible somewhere; the surface where the wine bottles are is not ideal.

TASTING SHEETS

Except for blind tastings, the more information on these the better: date, location, wine names and vintages in full are essential; prices optional, and enough space to write a note in! Clipboards are useful to write on, if awkward to store. **Most important** is that the order of wines on the tasting sheet is the same as that of the bottle line up, otherwise all sorts of confusion results.

DECANTING, POURING

Decanting is essential for blind tastings (into unlabelled bottles) and for any wines that contain a deposit. It is not fair to give the first two-thirds of a tasting group a clear, bright wine, and the last third an increasingly murky sample as the bottom of the bottle is reached. A narrow lipped jug is the most practical one for pouring the decanted wine back into its own bottle after the latter has been rinsed.

Pouring with a strip of tissue around the neck of the bottle helps prevent drips. After a little practice you will find you can comfortably get 20-22 tasting samples from a 75cl bottle if cost so demands. Where people are helping themselves, providing they *know* they have to be modest, I have generally found they take even smaller samples than when being served.

TASTING ORDER AND TEMPERATURE

Order: dry before sweet; white before red (although preferences vary here); light before heavy; lesser before finer; young before old. There is no perfect order, and occasionally compromises will have to be made. (Do you serve a much lighter, older vintage after a younger, strong and heady one?) Finally, it is worth remembering that at a stand up tasting or when faced with a choice of several glasses, nobody *has* to taste the wines in their presented order, they can please themselves.

Temperature is always tricky. I think the most important thing to remember is that wine will inevitably warm up in the glass, and that it is better to serve it on the cooler rather than the warmer side, reds included. Ideal temperature is a matter of taste to some extent and the glass can always be warmed in one's hands. If people are helping themselves, white wines can be kept cold in a "vinicool" or buckets with ice and water, although the latter tend to be very messy.

HINDRANCES

There are three things that can upset or distort one's impressions.

Smells Tobacco smoke and men's or women's perfumes. Though one's nose adapts rapidly to surrounding odours, these are inconsiderate and certainly intrusive.

Foods Chocolate and egg usually coat the taste buds so that they can't taste anything else properly. Any hot, strong, spicy or persistent flavour dulls perception and is thus inimical to effective tasting: mint, eucalyptus, pepper and so on.

Other tasters' comments Keep your impressions to yourself until others ask for them – mmm's, ah's and grimaces included. Nothing is so destructive to one's confidence as someone else's forcefully voiced and very different opinion before you have even finished.

WHEN TO TASTE

Ideal tasting times are before a meal, when the prospect of wine seems appetizing. Eleven o'clock in the morning, or six o'clock in the evening are common times. If you don't like tasting on an empty stomach (and alcohol goes to your head quicker in this case), a large glass of milk, or water, and a plain sandwich are a good "base". If your alcohol tolerance is low, as mine is, plenty of water during a long tasting is also a very effective measure.

(continued from p.34)
litter or something similar at the bottom. Where it is practical, placing the spittoon on a table (at waist rather than floor level) makes for a better hit rate and fewer stained skirts, stockings or trousers. Where you have fabrics (carpet, tablecloth) to protect, plastic bags beneath the spittoons serve well. Biscuits: small, plain and dry. The less crumbly the better (water biscuits are best). Water: tap or non-fizzy bottled.

(**Left, above**) *There are commercial "collars" that you can purchase to prevent drips when pouring; I find a paper towel tied round the bottle neck is just as effective.*

UNDERSTANDING TASTE: **SWEETNESS, ACIDITY, BITTERNESS AND ASTRINGENCY**

Anyone bitten by the wine bug beyond sheer hedonism, will sooner or later be asking themselves "Why?". A profound interest in any subject seeks explanations for why things are the way they are; curiosity is part of the appeal, curiosity satisfied part of the pleasure. Some idea of what accounts for the different tastes and varying balances in wine will satisfy that curiosity when it comes to interpreting sensations, rationalizing judgements, attempting to project a wine's future and so on. The following sections deal with where the tastes come from and how they interact with each other, how they "balance".

The key to good wine is good grapes, to well balanced wine, well balanced grapes. After flowering the grape develops into a hard green bead containing the equivalent of about 20g/l of sugar and 20g/l of acid, (tartaric and malic in about equal proportions) and it tastes unbearably sour. (Roughly 30g/l of sugar are reckoned to "balance" 1g/l of tartaric acid.) As it

ripens it gains sugar principally by photosynthesis and consumes acid for nourishment, malic acid in particular. When the grape is "ripe" it will contain roughly 200g/l of sugar, glucose and fructose in equal parts; and about 6g/l of acid, three-quarters tartaric, one-quarter malic (the hotter the climate the more malic is consumed). The exact proportions at picking will depend on the grape variety, the region, the year's weather pattern and on the style of wine required; but the "balance" in the grape when it is picked will be reflected in the finished wine.

The sugar/acid balance is the main, but not the only deciding factor in when to harvest. Physiologically fruit is ripe when it has attained its maximum amount of sugar, but this is not necessarily the moment when the winemaker will want to harvest. In the case of white grapes he may want to harvest *earlier* in order to preserve a little more acidity, and in the case of aromatic white varieties, because their aromatic optimum is reached before the sugar maximum. In the case of red grapes he may want to pick as *late* as possible because the tannins in the skin continue to improve in taste, texture and aroma for as long as the grape is ripening. But the longer he waits the less acidity the grapes will have, and a red wine with lots of alcohol and fine, ripe tannin is not much

(**Right**) *Grapes soon after flowering, just beginning to develop into the hard, green beads that will eventually become the ripe fruit.*

good if it has insufficient backbone. The question of balance starts in the vineyard.

SWEETNESS

From the grape *Fructose* and *glucose* are the main source of sweetness in sweet wines, being sugar that has not been fermented into alcohol, but even dry wines contain up to 2g/l of unfermented sugars, although this is not detectable as sweetness.

From fermentation *Alcohol* (ethyl alcohol) is the most important source of sweetness in dry wine. Although it doesn't have an obviously sugary taste by itself, it functions as such, reinforcing what sweet flavours there are, and softening the impressions of acidity, and tannin* if present. (As we have seen, alcohol also contributes to impressions of body or "thickness", and it helps support and bring out aroma and bouquet.) *Glycerol*, a by-product of the fermentation of glucose, tastes as sweet as glucose, but its content in wine is rarely above its perception threshold of about 15g/l. The viscous appearance of *Glycerol* in its pure form suggests that it makes wines "smoother" and "richer", but controlled tastings have shown its only effect in wine to be on the overall impression of sweetness.

Sweetness and balance In addition to its taste, sweetness makes a wine appear softer and richer by moderating acidity, astringency and bitterness. It prolongs the initial roundness on the palate by delaying the appearance of these harsher impressions. Excess sweetness in sweet wines will mask the acidity and make the wine appear too soft, and lacking in definition; syrupy or cloying in extreme cases. Excess sweetness in dry wines is likely to be due to too much alcohol, in which case, as well as not tasting as "dry" as they should, they also tend to be heavy, ponderous and hot. Excessive alcohol in dry white wines can also accentuate bitterness.

ACIDITY

From the grape *Tartaric* and *malic*. Tartaric acid is wine's principle acid both in terms of quantity and strength. Malic acid is "greener" in taste and clashes with tannin in a way that tartaric doesn't, hence the need to eliminate malic acid via malolactic fermentation in tannic red wines. In hot regions the ripe grape will contain little malic acid; in more temperate regions just how much it contains will depend on the weather pattern. Where it is present in the final wine, the winemaker can choose to leave it, or to eliminate it totally or partly by malolactic fermentation (qv). *Citric* acid is largely eliminated during the course of fermentation, although it may be added to the finished wine as a corrective. When this occurs, the wine often tastes "citric"; as in many white wines from Australia for example.

From fermentation *Succinic* acid, present in a small quantity, but with a complex flavour: acidic, salty and bitter, contributing to a wine's vinosity. *Lactic* acid, produced from the bacterial fermentation of malic acid (malolactic fermentation). Lactic acid is a softer, less aggressive acid than malic and marries better with tannin in red wines. *Acetic* acid is a "volatile" acid (it can be smelled). All the previous acids are "fixed" (they do not smell). All wines contain about 0.4–0.6g/l of acetic acid, at which level it can neither be smelled nor tasted. In excess it is a fault (qv), for it then smells vinegary and tastes sour.

Acidity and balance Acidity is the backbone of a wine without which it would be shapeless. It defines a wine's flavour, supports its finish and aftertaste, enlivens its appearance and acts as a natural preservative. Acid modifies and diminishes sweetness but it

* One of the principle reasons for chaptalizing (qv) red wines.

(**Left**) *The remarkably thick crust of crystalized tartaric acid that forms on the inner walls of vats used to store white wine . . . Alsace wine in this case. Once it is hammered off, it ends up being ground into cream of tartar for the kitchen.*

accentuates tannin. Thus the sweeter or more alcoholic, and the less tannic a wine is, the more acidity it needs and the more it can stand. Conversely, the more tannic the wine the less acid it requires, and the less it can support and still remain balanced. *Excess acid* makes a wine lean, hard, acidic; it also diminishes its bouquet. *Inadequate acid* makes for wines that lack freshness, relief and finish; wines that are dull, flat, flabby, shapeless.

Acids and age Fixed acids decrease with age, so softening the wine. Tartaric acid in particular combines with other components to make insoluble crystals which then precipitate. Volatile acid (acetic acid, vinegar) increases with age, making the wine harsher and "drier". However, in both cases the process is very gradual.

BITTERNESS AND ASTRINGENCY
From the grape These are both due to *tannins*, one of a group of phenolic substances, the best of which come from the skin of the grape. There is very little tannin in white wines and the following comments refer to red wines in particular. Bitterness, found predominantly in young, tannic wines, is just one of the flavours produced by tannin, but tannin is not necessarily bitter unless the grapes are unripe or the tannin content coarse and excessive. Bitterness is exacerbated by high acidity and/or high alcohol.

Apart from colour, tannin also affects smell, taste and touch. Good quality tannin (from "noble" grape varieties and ripe grapes) will contribute much to the wine's aroma, and to its savour, quite apart from the astringency of texture with which it is generally asso-

ciated. Astringency is nevertheless its most significant attribute where the balance of a wine is concerned.

Tannic astringency and balance The *degree* of astringency varies considerably according not only to the quantity of the tannin, but to its quality. Alcohol and sweetness modify and soften the effect of astringency, delaying its perception on the palate. High acidity accentuates its effect and accelerates its perception as astringency on the palate. Red wines with lots of tannin do not need as much acidity as those with very little tannin because their tannin both "shapes" and preserves them. The less tannic red wines are, the more their structure resembles that of white wines, and the more acidity they require to give them definition and appeal. Wines like Beaujolais Nouveau have barely any tannin, but a refreshing acidity instead, and, resembling a white wine in all but colour, they are also drunk in a similar fashion . . . cool.

Tannin and age Like acidity, tannin is a natural preservative in red wines and it is predominantly responsible for the way in which they age and develop. The following explanation is a very simplified version of a current theory on tannin and its function. The astringent character of tannin comes from the ability of its molecules to combine with the protein molecules in our saliva, "coagulating" it, destroying its lubricating character and so producing the puckering effect on our gums. (You get an impressive, if unsavoury, visual demonstration of tannin's coagulating properties when you have thoroughly rinsed your mouth with a red wine and spat it into a basin.)

The *extent* of astringency, gently drying or

(Right) A highly simplified, diagrammatic representation of how tannin varies in its astringent affect according to its chemical structure, 1, 2 and 3 represent three different wines of the same quality containing an equivalent quantity ot tannin. Although they have the same amount of tannin, their astringency will vary because of the tannin's varying chemical structure. In wine 1 the "four" tannin molecules are not yet "polymerized" and its texture is soft. In wine 2 they have polymerized into two larger units of two and the wine's texture is moderately tannic. In wine 3 the same notional weight of four molecules has now combined into one very large single unit and the wine is very bitter and astringent (first peak on graph opp.). But at some stage (ill defined as yet), further enlargement of the tannin molecules is no longer accompanied by a corresponding increase in astringency and the wine begins to soften ("maturity plateau" on graph), before it finally gains in astringency once more as it "dries out" (see second peak on graph, and text).

Noble grapes from better sites and soils will have a finer textured tannin to start with, but the way in which the wine develops in bottle will follow a similar progression.

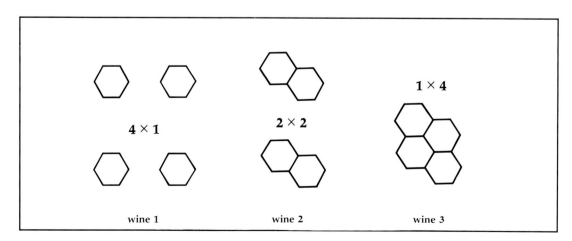

extremely puckering, is linked to the tannin's polymerization. This is the uniting of single molecules of the same substance to produce larger molecules ("mers") which themselves combine to produce polymers. The bigger the molecule, the stronger its capacity to combine with saliva protein and the greater its astringent effect. Thus *for the same quantity of tannin, the quality of astringency will vary* according to its degree of polymerization. Polymerization progresses continually as the wine ages, so that tannic wines for long ageing become gradually **harder** *to begin with.* (They taste *more* tannic after a few years in bottle than they did in barrel, see graph below.)

However, this is only to begin with, for at a very high degree of polymerization, the extra large molecules *lose* their ability to combine with protein and

their astringency *diminishes* though their sapid character is retained. At the same time they are combining with other components in the wine, becoming insoluble and precipitating to form the characteristic deposit, i.e. some tannin is being lost. At this stage the wine is in its mature, mellow phase; softer, richer, rounder: the "maturity plateau" (see graph).

Later still the increasingly large polymers gather strength once more and become drily astringent again. This effect is made more apparent as the wine is then also losing its fruit and gaining in volatile acidity; it is "drying out". Science is fairly confident about explaining the initial hardening phase of tannin, less so about explaining its subsequent mellowing and still puzzled by the drying out phase. All three are a physical reality on the palate (see diagram and graph).

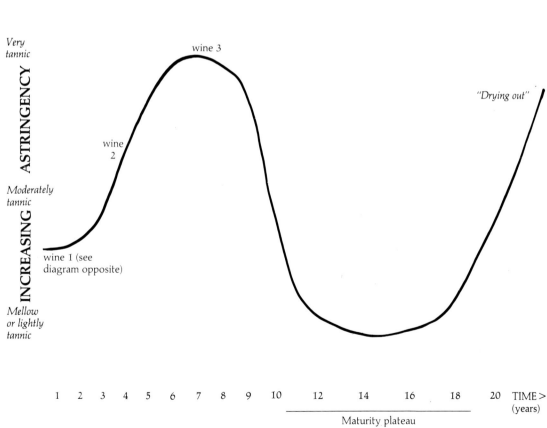

This graph represents the typical rise, fall and rise in tannic astringency of a good vintage, classed growth Médoc over about two decades. The wine gets harder in bottle to begin with before it softens into its maturity plateau; it then gradually becomes drily astringent again, an effect which is exacerbated because the wine is losing its fruit; it is "drying out".

TIME IN YEARS

UNDERSTANDING TASTE: FAULTS

Winemaking is of such a high standard today that faults are relatively uncommon. They do exist however, and whether you are returning a bottle in a restaurant, to a retailer or just wondering what a strange smell is, you should find most of the answers here. The two largest groups of faults are oxygen related faults, and sulphur related faults.

OXYGEN AND OXYDATION

Oxidized in a wine context means *over*-oxidized as oxygen is a natural component of wine and beneficial, in small quantities, to its maturation.

Oxidized white wines lack freshness, smell flat, and possibly of **acetaldehyde** (a stale, heavy, slightly pungent aroma vaguely similar to that of Amontillado sherry — although a sherry nose is the fresh and buttery-nutty smell of "rancio", with acetaldehyde being a part of its style). They taste flat and tired, and in colour are dull straw to brown. This characteristic appearance (and smell) has given rise to the term **maderized**, ie Madeira-like in colour, for heavily oxidized white wines. The term "maderized" is not used for reds, and tends to be reserved for heavily oxidized whites.

Oxidized red wines Although acetaldehyde is first in the oxydation chain, red wines rarely smell of it because it combines with their colour pigments and tannin. In the early stages of oxydation red wines, like whites, just smell and taste rather flat, maybe stale, with a touch of bitter-sweet caramel character and they are said to be **oxydized**.

As both red and white wines deteriorate further they begin to smell of the next stage of oxydation: acetic acid (vinegar). Because acetic acid is the "volatile" acid, this stage is more precisely described as *volatile* ("pricked" is a vivid, if more old fashioned term for the same thing), the wine smells "sweet and sour" initially, finally just sour and vinegary. Volatile acidity makes a wine taste thin, hard, sour with the finish being sharp and acrid.

At this stage the wine may also smell of ethyl acetate, very similar to nail varnish. Ethyl acetate is linked to the production of acetic acid, but not in direct proportion; hence a red wine can smell of either, or of both at once; although one is usually dominant. Where ethyl acetate dominates it makes sense to indicate this by describing the wine as *acescent* (as distinct from volatile) as the French do. Excess ethyl acetate makes the palate hard and dry, and noticeably hot on the finish.

Clearly "oxydized" covers all three of these conditions, but by itself it is imprecise.

SULPHUR

There are two quite distinct types of "sulphur-fault" smells, one comes from an excess of *sulphur dioxide* (SO_2), sulphur combined with oxygen; the other from *hydrogen sulphide*, (H_2S), sulphur combining with hydrogen in the absence of oxygen; this is "reduced" sulphur, producing "reduced" smells.

Sulphur dioxide (SO_2) Free sulphur dioxide is volatile, ie sulphur in a gas state. In excess it has a sharp, pungent smell and after a strong sniff it can be sensed as a pungent pricking at the top of one's nose, and a "catching" at the back of the throat. (Try smelling the whiff from a safety match immediately after

PROGRESSIVE OXYDATION OF "OXYDIZED" WINES, showing the variety of faults caused by excess contact with oxygen (O_2)

Cause (simplified)	Symptoms	Fault Description
O_2 + Alcohol ----------------- >Acetaldehyde: – (white wine)	Dull straw to brown colour. Flat/stale; unpleasant sherry-like smell and similar taste.	Maderized (white wine) (= oxydized)
O_2 + Alcohol ----------------------------------- : – (red wine)	Browner colour. Flat/stale; possibly bitter-sweet and/or caramelly smell and taste.	Oxydized (red wine)
O_2 + Acetaldehyde and/or O_2 + Acetic Bacteria } ----- > Acetic Acid: –	Dominated by the sour smell of the "volatile" acid, *Acetic Acid* (vinegar); thin and sharp to taste.	Volatile (VA for short) or pricked (red and white wine)
Acetic acid + Alcohol -------- > Ethyl Acetate: – (The ester of Acetic Acid)	Dominated by the nail varnish or strong pear drop smell of *Ethyl Acetate:* dry and hot to taste.	Acescent (Red and white wines)

(**Left**) *Scruffy cellars like this one don't necessarily mean that the wines won't be good, however the odds are obviously higher in that direction. Casks that are not properly maintained inside, whatever their appearance from without, will produce casky, woody wines.*

(**Lower left**) *Sulphur tablets. After periodic racking, when the barrels are cleaned of a wine's sediment, the little pale yellow tablets on the ends of these rods are lit and then suspended from the barrel's bung hole. As the sulphur burns slowly it fumigates and sterilizes the inside of the barrel. Sulphur is the most common antiseptic used in winemaking; used sensibly it is harmless and undetectable. Used carelessly it creates unpleasant faults.*

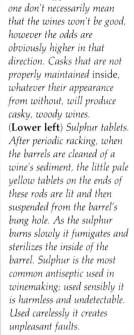

lighting and before you extinguish it when it will just smell of burnt wood.) Generally if sulphur dioxide can be *smelled* on a wine it can also be detected on the finish where it feels acrid and prickly at the back of one's throat. Most often noticed on opening a bottle and in the first glass, it can be dissipated by generous swirling. People's sensitivity to sulphur dioxide varies enormously.

Hydrogen sulphide (H$_2$S) Hydrogen sulphide is more common in wine before bottling, usually as a result of yeast activity in the "reduced" conditions of fermentation. In bottled wine it is a more evil smell than sulphur dioxide, reminiscent of bad eggs, rubber, stink bombs! If it is allowed to remain in young wine for too long it will combine with other components to form *mercaptans*, much more difficult to remove, and smelling pungently of garlic and stale sweat. In very extreme cases even fouler smelling *disulfides* will be formed – which smell like sewage!

Bottle stink A mild and short lived "reduced" smell which wears off after a brief aeration. Decanting will usually get rid of it. If it is *not* short lived it is one of the more sinister hydrogen sulphide smells.

CORKED/CORKY

Not broken fragments of cork in the wine. Corked wines smell particularly of *mould*, sometimes accompanied by suggestions of rotting undergrowth or dustiness. The latest theory is that corkiness is due not to moulds themselves, but to moulds in the cork being attacked by chlorine compounds in the sterilizing solutions!

CASKY/WOODY

The smell of old, damp, rotting wood and dank cellars. On the palate the wines have a similar dirty taste and often a coarse astringency. The cause is, not surprisingly, casks that are either too old, or which haven't been properly cleaned and maintained.

UNDERSTANDING TASTE:
SOIL, SITE AND CLIMATE

SOIL

Of course soil is important. However, its significance is much more for the grower as a basis for successful vine growing than it is for the drinker in terms of recognizing and enjoying what is in the glass. The grower needs to know what vines are best suited to the soil he has in the region where he lives; but from one wine growing country to another there is little correlation between particular soils and quality of wine or its particular characteristics.

Received wisdom is that sand produces light, quickly maturing wines; chalk yields supple wines with an exalted varietal character; gravel provides finesse; clay a heavier, firmer style. This is true in only the most general way. And whereas I can dip my nose into a glass and take pleasure in recognizing a Cabernet style and flavour, be it from Bordeaux, Bulgaria or Chile (and if I know the property there is added enjoyment to be had from associations with the place, people and occasions) I very rarely say to myself: "that brings back memories of calcareous clay with an overlay of limestone . . . Mmmmm!" I do sometimes make a more general comment about an "earthy" or "minerally" character in the wine though. (See Riesling, Chenin, Cabernets Sauvignon and Franc, Syrah and Keknyelü.)

Even if you know the soil of a given vineyard, what you see on the surface is a very limited reflection of the complex underlying geology. Although the relationship between vine roots and their habitat is a crucial one, and certainly accounts in part for differences in style and quality, for all the ink expended on it the precise link between soil, quality and flavour is not easy to identify in the wine.

SITE

The closer a vineyard is to the limits of vinegrowing (a northerly latitude in the northern hemisphere, a southerly one in the southern hemisphere), the more details such as slope and aspect matter in order for the vines to get maximum benefit from the sun's warmth and minimum exposure to wind or frost. On the open plains of France's southern Rhône or Midi, a southerly aspect is not that crucial, in Chablis it makes all the difference between plain "Chablis" and "Chablis Premier Cru". Similarly, the further north the site (in the northern hemisphere), the more beneficial a steep slope for concentrating the sun's rays.

Proximity to water in such locations is often a useful temperature regulator, maintaining a slightly higher average and minimizing the effect of marked changes (vineyards on the banks of the Gironde in Bordeaux, or the Rheingau vineyards close to the Rhein in Germany). And where "noble rot" is sought, an adjacent lake or river encourages misty mornings

(**Below**) *Quality wines can be produced on numerous different soils. What matters is that the vines grown are well suited to the soil. Knowing the soil type sometimes explains part of a wine's style or quality, but exceptions abound.* (**Top to bottom, from left to right**) *Some generalizations: a lighter, quicker maturing style of wine comes from this sandy soil in Margaux. Gravelly soil in St Julien yields a particularly refined wine. Clay drains slowly and is relatively cold; in Bordeaux it doesn't permit Cabernet Sauvignon to ripen soon enough, but Merlot thrives in it, as in Pomerol (bottom row). Appearances can be deceptive: the Châteauneuf stones may mask clay, sand or gravel, and ploughing shows a very different subsoil below this chalky Sancerre surface.*

in autumn, essential for its development. Valley floors or nearby woods on the other hand will encourage freezing air to sit and so expose the vines to frost.

But for the wine bibber, as opposed to the technician or vineyard owner, what are probably of more interest are vineyards as places: depicted in prose, mirrored in photographs or, richer still, recalled from visits in person, so that a wine stirs the memory, evoking scents, scenes, people and occasions – experiences far beyond immediate pleasures in the glass.

CLIMATE

The warmer and sunnier a wine region the less variation there is likely to be in style and quality from year to year, and the less "vintage" matters. But the quicker the grape ripens, as it does under such conditions, the less intense and clear cut its varietal character. Where the minutiae of annual temperature, hours of sunshine and inches of rainfall matter more particularly are, as with slope and aspect, in the more northerly European vineyards. Here, in years of suffi-

cient warmth and sunshine these "cooler" conditions permit the long, slow ripening of the grapes that produce the maximum flavour and the most exalted and refined qualities in wine.

Cooler conditions can be achieved in warm climates by siting vineyards at latitudes further from the equator, at higher altitudes, with aspects that avoid the midday sun, or near cooling stretches of water. In this way the generally "hotter" climates of Australia and the Americas for example, can produce wines that equal the refinement of many European vineyards, albeit in a different style.

*Two northerly vineyards where aspect is crucial: (**Above**) The Rudesheimer Berg in Germany's Rheingau, looking over the Rhein to Bingen. A south facing slope maximizes exposure to the sun, and the proximity of a large expanse of water acts as a temperature regulator. (**Inset**) Looking due north over Chablis vineyards. Those in the foreground face north and benefit from less sun; they are plain Chablis. Those on the other side of the valley face south; they are Premier Cru Chablis. The soil is the same; aspect makes the difference.*

The best known oaks are those from France and the southern United States. American oak is the cheapest, most widely available wood and it has the sweetest, most obvious vanilla character. It is the one generally used for Rioja. Of the French oaks, that from Nevers in central France is the slowest growing, most close grained and tends to give a firmer, drier texture to the wine than the quicker growing, more open grained oak from the Limousin or Tronçais forests further to the southwest.

(Right) *Oak ageing is fashionable (this will change!). Here Pascal Delbeck of Château Ausone is experimenting with "oaking" a lowly Entre Deux Mers.*
(Opposite) *Barrelmaking in Australia. Heat helps bend the staves and naked flames "char" the inside of the barrel. This gives a distinctive taste to the wine and careful winemakers regulate the charring to produce the flavour appropriate for their wine.*

UNDERSTANDING TASTE: CARBON DIOXIDE, OAK AND BOTTLE AGE

CARBON DIOXIDE (CO₂)

We normally associate carbon dioxide bubbles with champagne and other sparkling wines, but it is a significant component of still wines even when invisible. Carbon dioxide combined with water produces carbonic acid (H_2CO_3), the very mild tasting acid which we all know from carbonated water and fizzy drinks.

The main source of carbon dioxide is fermentation, after which it can be deliberately retained in the wine, or eliminated to the desired extent by racking (qv). As an additional acid, carbon dioxide doesn't marry well with tannin in red wines; and the more tannic they are, the less carbon dioxide they will contain.

Most white wines to be drunk young contain up to half a gram of carbon dioxide per litre. At or below this level it is neither visible nor perceptible on the tongue, but it noticeably affects appearance, nose and flavour. Its presence enlivens a wine's colour, gives the bouquet a lift and makes the palate taste fresher and longer on the finish. Wines which have a few bubbles visible in the glass will probably have a slight initial prickle on the tip of the tongue. Many young, straightforward whites from warmer climates have a perceptible amount of carbon dioxide to give them a bit of added zip.

The amount of carbon dioxide present in basic white wines, and the adverse effect of too little can be convincingly demonstrated in a simple experiment. Take a bottle of inexpensive white from Italy, southern France, Australia or California for example, and decant a third of the wine into another bottle. With your thumb over the top of this second bottle, shake it vigorously in order to eliminate as much of the carbon dioxide as possible. You may have to do this for a couple of minutes or more, releasing your thumb occasionally to let the accumulated gas escape. You will be surprised at the "head" that builds up! Put both bottles in the fridge for an hour or more to let the "shaken" one settle and to bring them both to the same temperature again. When you taste them side by side you will find the wine with little carbon dioxide is not as brilliant to look at, smells duller, and tastes flatter, less well defined and shorter on the palate.

OAK

Ageing red or white wines in new oak barrels, or barrels that have only had wine in them for a year or two, has a marked effect on bouquet, and texture. The most obvious characteristic on the nose is the smell of vanilla, from the vanillin in the wood. As the wine ages, other sweet and fragrant smells appear as the result of chemical combinations; that of "cedar" or "cigarbox" in cabernet based wines, is one of the spicier varieties. On the palate, in addition to the vanillary aroma, tannin from new oak gives a firmer, drier and more complex texture, one which brings out other flavours and which provides a sharper definition to the wine; rather like a slightly soft picture being brought into crystal clear focus. In contrast to the "thicker" astringency of grape tannin, the feel of new oak tannin is a pronounced, somewhat spicy and fine grained "dryness". The best way to appreciate its effect is to taste different samples of the same young wine at a winery, one from new barrels, one from old; or a "straight" and an "oak-aged" Bulgarian Cabernet or Chardonnay as both styles are now available.

Oak charring When barrels are fashioned the

staves are "bent" over a fire and as a result the inside is "charred" to some extent. This charring can be exaggerated to give red wines a more "smoky" character, and white wines a more "toasty" one (freshly toasted bread).

Extent of oak ageing In general, the more full bodied and more concentrated a wine the more oak ageing it can stand. Too long in exclusively new oak makes a wine excessively dry and harsh, and the vanilla character overwhelming. This is particularly noticeable in a wine not intended for extended maturation in bottle, which would allow the oakiness to mellow and integrate. White wines which have spent too long in oak can also take on a bitter, resinous taste in addition to the excess astringency. Curiously, white wines that are *fermented* as well as *aged* in new barrels are usually less obviously vanillary and less astringent than those that are bulk fermented and only aged in oak. One theory to explain this is that yeasts present during the fermentation "fine" (qv) the wood tannin to some extent.

BOTTLE AGE

When is a wine "mature"? There is no simple answer. It depends on the wine and also on your taste. Most wines are made to be drunk young, within a year or two of being made, and in the United Kingdom at least, more wines are probably drunk too old than too young. A hangover from the time when wine drinking was largely confined to the·wealthier, and consisted principally of claret, port and burgundy which required years of ageing in the cellar before drinking. Wines that need keeping will taste unintegrated, that is you will be able to sense their component parts as distinctly separate, particularly in respect of acid and tannin. As they age, such wines undergo a slow process of chemical combination which enriches their bouquet and flavour, and mellows their texture as those very components needed to keep them decrease and soften, and can no longer be perceived as obtrusively separate elements, but as a married whole.

When is "ready"? When you like it, is when it's ready! There is no more a perfect age for wine than there is for people; their appeal is different at different stages. In youth they can be enjoyed for their vigour and emphatic fruit, especially with food which will mask some of the harsher edges; in old age what they lack in strength they make up for with suppleness of texture, subtlety of flavour and increased bouquet. Which stage you prefer them at, and the degree to which you like tannin or acid to be apparent are matters of culture and individual taste.

GRAPES AND THEIR WINES

In this section I deal with specific wines and give you an idea of what to look for in comparable wines from different countries and thus provide a starting point from which to judge and appreciate them.

White wines, dry and sweet, are dealt with first followed by red, sparkling and fortified wines. Finally there is a section on spirits. For each type there is an outline of winemaking and then an exploration of the category by grape variety.

An orange or lemon, peach or pear is recognizable as such from its smell, taste and texture wherever it comes from. The common denominator of a grape variety might suggest that wines from different places should be similarly recognizable; but this is far from the case. And if it were wine would not be the fascinating subject that it is. The varietal link often seems very tenuous. Not only due to variations in clone and climate, but also because expectations of what wine from a particular grape variety should taste like vary from one country to another. This in turn affects the winemaker's aims and winemaking process.

An understanding of what lies behind the smells, tastes and textures in the glass helps account for one's impressions, adds to one's pleasure or explains disappointment. The principal factors that affect style and quality are outlined in the sections on winemaking.

For each grape variety or style I have tried to describe the most typical characteristics of balance, aroma, texture and flavour that you can expect of its wines from around the world. I have selected what I consider to be quintessential examples from each area, and suggested certain comparisons which, tasted next to each other, will highlight differences in style. Any of these comparisons should give you a good idea of the range and variety that lies behind just one grape name, even if you do not agree with my opinions. For, I cannot pretend to be absolutely objective. Your tastes will often differ from mine, and the comments that I have made will be but stimulus for your own.

Trying to clarify the differences between the wines you taste, and explaining or justifying your own preferences will develop your tastes (and tasting ability), deepen your understanding and, most of all, enhance your enjoyment of what is in your glass. It has done so with me, and that is what this book is all about.

The grape varieties are arranged in their order of importance, in this section. To find a particular variety, you should refer to the Index.

One bunch of ripe grapes looks much like another on the vine. But, wherever it is transformed into quality wine its smells, tastes and textures will have a quite distinct personality, whose characteristics remain recognizable whatever the local accent or national dress.

(**Right**) *A modern grape
"crusher". Crushing is a
misnomer ("milling" is the
more popular current term).
The aim is simply to break the
skins to let the juice run; if the
skins or pips are bruised the
wine will taste coarser. The
counter-rotating rollers are
now usually made of rubber,
and are only just close enough
to split the grapeskins.*

(**Below, right**) *Crucial
decision. A winemaker in the
northern Rhône using a
refractometer (which indicates
the level of sugar in the
grape's juice) to help him
decide when to pick. He will
take many measurements
from grapes in different parts
of the vineyard to get a
sampling of how ripe the
crop is.*

FERMENTATION
The basic chemical reaction, common to all wines
during fermentation is:
**Yeasts convert sugars to alcohol + carbon
dioxide**
In white wine the juice of the grapes is fermented by
itself, not in contact with the skins as happens with
red wines.

DRY WHITE WINEMAKING

When to pick the grapes is the winemaker's most
crucial decision. However good his winemaking techniques, the quality of the resulting wine will reflect the
quality and qualities of the grapes when harvested.
The problem for a winemaker in the cooler climatic
areas is to get sufficient ripeness in the slow maturing
fruit before the weather changes. With unripe grapes
he can add sugar to gain more alcohol (chaptalization)
and he can "de-acidify" juice that is too sour, but he
cannot make up for the lack of flavour.

The winemaker in the hotter areas has no difficulty
in ripening his fruit and achieving satisfactory levels

of sugar; but these grapes may also lack flavour and
aroma precisely because they have ripened *too*
rapidly, and his main problem is to procure ripe
grapes with sufficient acidity. Just as the cool climate
winemaker can de-acidify, the hot climate winemaker
can "acidify" the wine, but this often tastes like
"added" acid, particularly if citric acid is used, as it can
give the wine a distinct "lemony/limey" sharpness. A
possible alternative is to pick part of the harvest
earlier, with more acid, vinify separately and then
blend the two wines.

From the moment the grapes have been picked, up

to the moment the wine is bottled, one of the white winemaker's primary concerns is to prevent the juice, the must or the finished wine from oxydizing. This hazard is worse in hot climates because the rate of oxydation increases considerably as temperature rises, and today the byword is "temperature-control".

Crushing This is too brutal a description for what is merely breaking the skin of the grapes so that they can be pressed to release their juice more efficiently. After this stage, before pressing, the crushed grapes are sometimes transferred to a vat to allow the partially freed juice to remain in contact with the skins for a day or two so as to draw out the aromas and flavour elements lying just below the skin; a limited maceration in effect. The grapes must be kept very cold to stop fermentation starting and they are usually kept under a blanket of inert gas to prevent oxydation. If contact is excessive tannins are also picked up and the wine is likely to be coarse and astringent.

Pressing When the grapes are transferred to the press, about a third of the available juice will be "free-run", and light pressing will express a further third. This juice is the best for winemaking and is often fermented separately. Further pressing will yield a juice that is coarser and more astringent as it extracts more tannins from the skins. The finally expressed juice can be used to make a separate wine, or one which can be used in part to blend back with the finer wine.

After a period of chilled settling which allows the must (as the juice is now called) to clarify, the acidity can be adjusted if necessary and fermentation can then begin.

Compare the taste and texture of three grapes: eat the flesh of the first *by itself*, the flesh of the second along with its skin very gently chewed – limited maceration – and with the third just keep on chewing the skin. This demonstrates how a *little* tannin can improve flavour and texture, but how the more you extract the coarser it gets and underlines how carefully crushing, pressing and maceration need to be monitored to avoid a coarse or astringent wine. White or red grapes will do, as the principle is just the same for red wines.

Fermentation may take place in small oak barrels for more expensive wines, otherwise in large cement or temperature controlled stainless steel vats. How long the fermentation takes will depend on the temperature at which it takes place.

*(**Above**) The creamy froth of gently fermenting white must in a non-stainless, resin lined metal vat.*
*(**Above left**) Low temperature fermentation is the key to fresh, aromatic white wines. Temperature in stainless steel vats is often controlled by running a stream of cold water over the sides, the water being re-cooled as required.*

TEMPERATURE AND "COLD FERMENTATION"

White wines fermented too fast, at too high a temperature, lose a lot of carbon dioxide and with it a lot of their aromas. At worst they can turn out heavy and flat as well. "Cold" fermentation means maintaining a temperature of 10°–15°C (50°–59°F) although it is often even colder. Why is this considered so important? The structure of light, dry white wines is fairly simple so that aromas and carbon dioxide matter. Cold fermentation is slow fermentation, with less bubbling loss of carbon dioxide, and hence a retention of volatile aromatic elements. At colder temperatures yeasts also produce a greater variety of primary, "fruity" aromas, thus cold fermentation wines are usually fresh, fruity and aromatic.

The minus side is that cold fermentation wines tend to taste alike wherever they come from. Cleanliness is frequently substituted for character. However, many of the heavier styles of dry white (Burgundy, Alsace) owe more to a greater extract for which a higher temperature is required – 18°–20°C (65°–68°F).

MALOLACTIC FERMENTATION (qv)

After alcoholic fermentation the winemaker may choose to eliminate all or some of any malic acid in the wine by malolactic fermentation. He will normally take steps to avoid malolactic fermentation in wines that need the acidity, or which are to be drunk young and which rely on a fresh, primary "aroma". Malolactic fermentation is generally encouraged however, in white wines that are destined for ageing in bottle, where the primary aroma, diminished after malolactic fermentation, is of less importance than the "bouquet" acquired in wood and/or bottle.

After fermentation(s) the wines may be *fined* to clarify them, and then bottled immediately after *filtering* or if they are to be aged they will then be put into vat, or, more likely, wooden barrels for varying periods of time before bottling.

(Top right, middle and bottom left) Filtering a white wine using Kieselguhr, diatomaceous earth like that used for talcum powder. The Kieselguhr is mixed to a slurry in the wine (top right) and it builds up on the outside of the circulating filter drum, creating an additional very fine filter barrier. It also acts to a limited extent as an electrochemical fining agent. The "before" and "after" glasses show just how effective it is. This is just one of numerous methods of filtering and fining.

(Bottom right) Oval wooden barrels in Alsace. Used to store wine before bottling. As the wood is old and heavily encrusted by tartrate crystals on the inside, it will not "flavour" the wine in the way new wood does, though it will allow it to age and mellow.

SWEET WHITE WINEMAKING

Sweet white wines are those with unfermented sugar in them (also known as residual sugar). Sweetness can vary from a few grams per litre in wines which are called off-dry or medium-dry (and which you think is the appropriate description is largely a matter of opinion), to intensely sweet wines such as German Beerenauslese, French Sauternes or Californian Late Harvest wines. The basic process of sweet white winemaking is as for dry white wine, but with additional procedures to make the wine sweet.

There are several means to obtaining wines with residual sugar in them.

Ferment until "dry" and add "sweet reserve" This method, originating in Germany, allows the winemaker to make the wine as sweet as he wants by adding sweet reserve to a dry wine just before bottling. Sweet reserve (süssreserve in German) is unfermented grape juice, pressed from the grapes, sterile filtered and kept very cold and under pressure (to prevent fermentation) until wanted.

Incomplete fermentation For grapes that are naturally very rich in sugar, fermentation can be stopped before all the sugar has been converted to alcohol. The crudest method of doing this is with a heavy dose of sulphur dioxide which renders the yeast inactive. (Most yeast will cease to "ferment" in any case at about 15° alcohol – but the precise degree at which they stop is too haphazard to rely on for good winemaking.) The method is becoming rarer, but it is unfortunately not yet extinct. Today it is more common to stop the fermentation by cooling the wine until the yeast are inactive and then removing them by centrifugation and sterile filtration. The other method of obtaining part fermentation is to knock out the yeast by adding alcohol in the form of grape brandy, this is called *fortification*.

The finest sweet white wines, however, are made from grapes that are "nobly rotten" or "botrytized" (from the name *Botrytis cinerea*).

(**Top left**) *A pressure meter indicating the intense compression (5–8 atmospheres) under which "süssreserve" is kept in order to prevent it fermenting. When drawn off, this intensely sweet, silky juice emerges as a mousse because it is so saturated with compressed air.*

(**Bottom left**) *A battery of "süssreserve" tanks in Germany. Each contains the unfermented juice of a different grape variety, vintage or quality category. For sweetening the finished wine the same quality "prädikat" (Kabinett, Spätlese, Auslese, etc.) is normally used. A better category is permitted but not an inferior one.*

(**Below**) *Sauternes must from botrytized grapes. This thick, murky syrup comes from the hardest pressing of the grapes which, in contrast to hard pressed non-botrytized grapes, yields the best quality juice.*

Botrytis cinerea *is a
greco-latin hybrid meaning an
"ash coloured bunch of
grapes", though it is better
known to most of us as the
disfiguring grey mould on
plants in our gardens. Its
effects may also be pernicious
in the vineyard; but it is one
of nature's more bizarre
anomalies that, under certain
conditions, the most
thoroughly rotten bunch of
grapes can produce the most
exquisitely luscious of sweet
white wines. The conditions
required for noble rot are
alternating periods of moisture
and dry warmth. Misty
mornings (**right**) and sunny
afternoons (**below**) are ideal,
as here at Ch. d'Yquem.*

NOBLE ROT

The requisite conditions for "noble rot" are that the grapes must be fully ripe and their skins must be intact, otherwise the juice, in contact with air, would turn to vinegar, in which case the rot would be "vulgar" rather than "noble". The autumn weather needs to provide alternating periods of gentle moisture to encourage the growth of the fungus, and sunny warmth to promote evaporation and concentration of the juice.

The locations most likely to produce these conditions are river valleys where autumn mists develop overnight and linger in the vineyards throughout the morning, lifting to blue skies and sunshine in the afternoon. The best vineyards for nobly rotten wines are: in France — Sauternes and Barsac on the river Garonne; Quarts de Chaumes and Bonnezeaux on the river Layon in Anjou; in Hungary — Tokay on the Bodrog; in Germany — the numerous vineyards of the Rhine and Mosel; and in Eastern Austria — on the banks of the Neusiedler See. In California and Australia the spores are sometimes sprayed onto ripe grapes on racks in specially insulated buildings, allowing controlled development of the rot.

The rotting process Spores settle on the grape skin and penetrate it via micro lesions, openings large enough to allow the fungus tentacles in (and out), but not large enough to expose the juice to the air. Inside the spores feed on the grape's sugars and particularly on its acids, at the same time creating new flavour-rich compounds. There is a decrease of sugars and acids in absolute terms, but the evaporation of water results in a concentration of all flavour elements except tartaric acid. In the very sweetest wines such as German Beeren- or Trockenbeeren-auslese and Tokay Essencia the must has such a high sugar content that the yeast can barely function. Fermentation may take many months, and even then the alcohol content may only reach 6°–8°.

As the rot does not develop at an even pace through the vineyard, successive pickings must be made of bunches or, for the finest wines, individual nobly rotten grapes, making these wines very expensive to produce. Concentration alone would simply make the wine thicker and sweeter, indeed this is what happens in a year where there is inadequate moisture for the botrytis to develop. (1978 Sauternes – d'Yquem and Guiraud are good examples.) It is the new compounds created by the botrytis which eventually make it also far more exotic to smell, and far more exciting to drink. I say eventually because botrytis "develops" in the bottle too. When young it gives the basic honey/barley sugar aroma of Sauternes (for example) a waxy, lanolin smoothness; but when mature, say at ten years for a good vintage, its bouquet is denser and more penetrating, redolent of roasted nuts and musk, sometimes with a hint of something vegetal too.

The rich, sweet flavour of mature nobly rotten wines is also subtler, racier and more spicily interesting. These characteristics appear in a lighter, livelier, but equally beguiling guise in Quarts de Chaumes and Bonnezeaux from the Loire; or as a layer to top the burnt caramel and butter bouquet in Hungarian Tokay, and as an intoxicating supplement to the heady, oily perfume of mature Riesling from the finest German Auslese and Beerenauslese.

The results of noble rot are seen, (smelled and tasted) at their best in wines made from Semillon (Bordeaux, Australia); Riesling (Germany especially); Chenin Blanc (Loire); Furmint (Hungary), and occasionally Gewürztraminer in Alsace (1976, 1983). There was even a fine botrytized Chardonnay from Burgundy in 1983: a Macon Clessé from Jean Thevenet.

(**Top left**) *Ripe, healthy Semillon grapes, on which the mist induced moisture will promote the growth of botrytis.*
(**Above**) *Seen under an electron microscope: the filaments of Botrytis cinerea emerging through a micro lesion on the grape's surface; these become the visible fungus.*
(**Centre left**) *The fungus develops slowly, initially as coppery stains, gradually colouring the whole skin sepia-pink to chocolate. A grey-brown fungus then starts to cover the surface, the grapeskin begins to wrinkle and shrink as the juice evaporates, and in the final stages it shrivels to a rotten looking raisin of extraordinary concentration.*
(**Bottom left**) *Botrytis spores developing in bottle at Beringer Winery, California. They will be used to develop "artificial" noble rot on already picked ripe grapes.*

CHARDONNAY

It is a curious fact that Chardonnay is both the most popular of the "classic" grape varieties for wine, and at the same time the one with the least identifiable personality on its own. When young and untouched by oak it doesn't have the easy-to-spot characteristics of a youthful Loire Sauvignon, clear cut and gooseberry like; the perfumed nose that signals an Alsatian Gewürztraminer, or the austere, faintly oily purity of dry Riesling, for example.

Pure Chardonnay, instead, is often identifiable only because it is *not* one of these. The nose is low key, reminding one of ripe fruit, apples possibly; with a bit more age there may be a suggestion of butter or nuts, but it is not a very clear declaration. On the palate it will be quite full and round, with a moderate acidity and a breadth that would say not Muscadet, not Chenin, nor Sauvignon or Riesling: it would be a negative identification, by elimination. But its unassertive character as a wine and undemanding nature as a vine make it the perfect cosmopolitan, readily adapting to the costumes and make up of locations around the globe. And Chardonnay's favourite costume is oak, a cloak to which it takes so well that "dry white wine plus oak" is practically synonymous with Chardonnay.

UNOAKED CHARDONNAY

For all that, unadorned Chardonnay does exist, mainly in Europe. Cheapest of the "ripe apple" wines are the modestly fruited, crisp and faintly earthy Bulgarian Chardonnays. Northeast Italy's product, from the South Tyrol in particular, is a broader, medium bodied wine, nut and apple on the nose, usually with a touch of spritz and best drunk within a year or two. Try those of Lageder and Tiefenbrunner.

FRANCE

In France the lightest representative is the Chardonnay du Haut Poitou; sharply refreshing, saying more about its Loire origins than its grape. Fuller and softer, with a little spritz, is the cold fermented Listel Chardonnay, from the sandy bay of the Golfe du Lion in Provence. Burgundian merchant Louis Latour's Chardonnay Latour hails from the wild Ardèche Valley where, having found a suitable chalky soil, he persuaded the local co-operative and their growers to replant and make the wine under his supervision. This is a full bodied, supple, more buttery style.

The southern and northern extremes of Burgundy, Mâconnais/Chalonnais and Chablis respectively, are where to look for archetypal, unoaked Chardonnay. In the Mâcon and Chalonnais region the finest wines from individual growers may use some wood, but the majority do not. The co-operatives are a reliable source, and any of the "village" wines from Pouilly or Mâcon will be an open, full bodied, attractively accessible wine. The Chardonnay clone in this region frequently has a distinctly sweet, honeyed nose, peachy-ripe in hot years, with an uncomplicated apples and melon fruit. In hot years like 1985 or 1983 they want drinking quickly, as their freshly-picked ripeness soon palls. In cooler years a zestier backbone may allow them to develop a little bottle age nuttiness on the nose, but on the whole they are not wines for keeping. Plain Mâcon typifies Burgundy's quality minefield: simple and delicious or unutterably dire.

(**Below**) *Chardonnay, the most popular white grape variety of all; which happily adapts to sites round the globe, but whose very finest wines still come from the Côte de Beaune in Burgundy.*

(**Left**) *Southern Burgundy's Pouilly Fuissé vineyards beneath the rearing form of the Solutré Rock in the Mâconnais; and (***below***) at Burgundy's northern extremity, the pale, limestone dominated slopes of Grand Cru Chablis (Bougros and Vaudésir). Both areas produce fine examples of unoaked Chardonnay.*

Pouilly-Fuissé, along with Rully from further north, can have a development to the palate and an aftertaste which put them closer to the fine whites of the Côte d'Or, although by this stage they are probably beginning to be touched by oak.

To confuse Mâcon with Chablis when tasting blind would seem to be an unlikely mistake. I assure you it is not! And it is precisely the absence of new-oak ageing that makes them confusible cousins. Add to this the current (and regrettable) tendency to make a softer, more forward and fruity style of Chablis, which also has a "boiled sweets" bouquet, and you can see why it is not so unlikely after all. Even so, most Chablis, new style or old, will have a nervier underlying acidity, and traditional Chablis is undoubtedly the purest and most refined expression of Chardonnay without make-up. Louis Michel's wines are the perfect illustration of this for his wines see no wood at all. They are fermented in stainless steel and bottled straight from the vat. They are not obvious or assertive wines, but his Premier and Grand Cru typify Chablis' vigorous constitution, its austere acidity and bone dry, minerally flavours.

Long live Chablis without new oak. In a sea of oak-vanilla sophistication we should be profoundly grateful for the relief provided by its small island of fine, unadulterated varietal character.

OAKED CHARDONNAY

I am certainly not saying that I don't care for the oakier versions. The key issue here is how much oak is too much? This is a question of "taste" in two senses. Firstly, vanilla is intrinsically appealing to most people and just how much you like is a question of individual preference; but a surfeit, like too much of anything, soon bores and offends the palate. Secondly, like any condiment, the point of oak is to improve or highlight a flavour. When it actually masks what it is designed to enhance it can no longer be justified on the grounds of style. It is clearly an imbalance that offends the aesthetic sense, not to say common sense as well.

Judiciously used, oak gives a subtle, almost creamy, vanilla topping to the grape aroma and an extra dimension of delicate spiciness to the taste; at the same time it adds a fine grained, racy definition to the texture. In young wine, even discreetly used, the oak will be palpable as such, but it will leave the wine's own flavours clearly perceptible too. In mature wine it becomes almost imperceptible as oak, contributing, in the case of Chardonnay, to the nuttiness or "toastiness" of its bouquet and to the complexity of mellow maturity. Overdone, oak's sweet vanilla taste and its dry spicy texture so dominate the wine that the flavour and aroma of the grape itself are totally lost.

There are excellent quality oaky Chardonnays from California, Oregon and Washington State in the Eastern United States; from Ontario in Canada, from Spain, Italy and Australia; and they encompass an enormous variety of styles. But Burgundy's Côte de Beaune remains a touchstone for balance.

The traditional distinctions between the wines from Puligny-Montrachet and Meursault are easy to make, perhaps less easy to justify. They are blurred by different styles of winemaking, even more by time, so that comparisons are best made with young wines. Puligny-Montrachet and Chassagne-Montrachet tend to be crisper, more tautly fine and racy than Meursaults, with flavours that tend to peach and tangerine. The more illustrious the wine the richer and more luscious it should be, all the while remaining "dry", and the longer it should develop on the palate and persist in aftertaste. These qualities ought to be found in any of the Montrachets: Chevalier-, Bâtard-, Bienvenue-Bâtard-Montrachet and Le Montrachet itself. If possible compare the styles of the same Puligny wines from different producers: for example Henri Clerc's are full and rich, sometimes lacking a little in race and definition; Domaine Leflaive's wines are all delicacy and refinement, those of Etienne Sauzet are a more vigorous style, somewhere in between.

Meursaults are often a slightly deeper colour, more suggestive of butter, nut or oatmeal on the nose; broader in constitution and with a softer more open texture. Lafon's wines are deep, silky and buttery; those of Guy Roulot firmer and with more "cut" to them, and the Meursaults of Bouchard Père et Fils interesting because they have a lower proportion of new oak.

The white Corton Charlemagne may not have the tingling raciness of the best Puligny-Montrachet wines, but it should be deep, broad and enveloping richly rich; a magnified, more complex version of Meursault perhaps. Bonneau du Martray's is one of the finest.

Vintage for white Burgundy is not as crucial for quality as it is for red (this is generally true of white wines) but it does affect the *style* of the wine much more than it does in the warmer, more regular climates of California and Australia for example. The 1980's have provided a particularly varied run of vintages. Comparisons are fascinating. To mention a few: the 1983's are vigorously great for the top wines, atypical in their weight of alcohol — almost California come to Burgundy — and flabby, lacklustre wines at

*(Below) The typical limestone soil in which Chardonnay thrives in the Côte de Beaune. This stony vineyard in Meursault is aptly named "Perrières", a good Premier Cru vineyard (along with "Genevrières" or "Charmes") to use in a comparison with a basic commune Meursault (**opposite**).*

worst. The 1982's are soft, pretty and elegant, but also watery in many cases. The 1984's may not have the richness and ripeness of 1983 or 1985, but the best have very clearly etched flavours as is often the case in "cooler" years; 1981 is another one of these, do not ignore them.

The majority of the Premier Cru and all the Grand Cru white burgundies will be marked by new oak. Look for the way in which it affects Chardonnay here; in most cases it is noticeably there but not excessive. Whilst it adds to and heightens flavours it doesn't dominate with vanillary sweetness or dry astringency – it feels integrated. To judge the effect of *old* wood on Chardonnay you could compare a Premier Cru Chablis of Michel again, or Durup (both no wood at all) with one from Albert Pic whose wines (pre-1987) spend a few months in old oak. Notice the way in which old wood subdues the "fruity" character of the grape on the nose, and how it is tasted as a faint "woody" astringency, but without any vanilla flavour.

CALIFORNIAN CHARDONNAY

Up until the late 1970's most Californian Chardonnay could fairly be summed up as overripe, overblown and dizzily alcoholic; usually with a hefty dose of oak and a "bouquet" of ripe pineapples. Critic and consumer resistance brought about an extreme swing of the style pendulum to wines that were lighter but also lean, green and charmless. The current style sits more contentedly in between. The wines are no longer so pineappley, but more minerally and earthy under a lighter oak vanilla; and their constitutions are firmer and less weighty.

The best wines are now between 12.5° and 13°. Californian Chardonnays indicate their alcoholic degree on the label, back or front, and sometimes their acidity too. Compare, if you can, wines of over and under 13°. Notice with the "over thirteens" how, if there is not enough fruit flavour to balance the alcohol they taste hot and hard; if there is inadequate acidity they taste dull, heavy and ponderous. Conversely,

(**Above**) *Looking northeast over Meursault from its "commune" vineyards. There are no Grand Crus in Meursault, but a comparison of the same producer's basic Meursault with a Premier Cru wine (**opposite**) from the same vintage, will illustrate the extra intensity and definition of flavour, development on the palate and length of aftertaste that distinguish the Premier Cru from the village wine. A Grand Cru from the commune of Puligny-Montrachet or Aloxe Corton would complete the quality hierarchy.*

with high alcohol *and* high acidity the combination becomes blunt and fierce, sometimes burning or bitter as the acid and alcohol reinforce each other. Where fruit and flavour are concerned, look not only for quantity, but for quality of interest; for "length" of flavour (development to the palate), aroma and aftertaste, the breed which is certainly to be found in the best Californian wines.

South of San Francisco, wines such as Chalone and Edna Valley (under the same management) are now usually under 13°. They are potent but not coarse. Chalone is a Californian Corton if you like, with great length and a pronounced aromatic character. Firestone is always reliable; a savoury, and beautifully balanced lightly oaked Chardonnay. North of San Francisco, the Napa Valley's byword for elegance and definition are Mondavi's wines. North of the Napa there are steelier examples like the crisp Mark West from Russian River Valley, or the elegant Matanzas Creek from Sonoma. Perhaps the most exciting pointer to future quality are some of the Chardonnays from cool Howell Mountain plateau to the east of the Napa Valley. Château Woltner's 1986 Titus Vineyard is truly something to vie with the French Montrachets. It has a flawless balance, refined and concentrated flavour, but most important of all, an abundance of aromatic interest on palate and aftertaste. And its lesser brethren are not far behind.

AUSTRALIA AND NEW ZEALAND

Australian Chardonnay has been riding high for several years now, but in a continent two thousand miles across, making wines at either extremity and for much of what lies between, it is no surprise to encounter at least as much indifferent as exceptional winemaking. As with Californian Chardonnay, what to look for is not white Burgundy, but balanced wine with an Australian personality, Australian interest, aromas and aftertaste as well – and some Chardonnay flavour!

What are the keys to Australian Chardonnay? To begin with a deep yellow colour. And if ripe pineapple used to be the trigger for a California nose, a similarly striking ripe fruit character shouts out Australia today, but it is grapefruit, grapefruit zest or similarly "citric" smells. There is an almost universal oak treatment (mainly American oak) which comes across as a sweet, candyfloss-cum-sherbet vanilla. The combination has often been called a tropical cocktail. The palate echoes the citrus theme of the nose, recalling lemon and lime. This aspect has become much more marked recently.

When Australian Chardonnays were first exported to any extent in the early eighties, they were ripe and juicy but seemed very soft at only a couple of years. The ability to keep and age is not necessarily a virtue, particularly in vibrantly fruity wines, but a noble

(**Right**) *Pinnacles, south of San Francisco in California. These are limestone hills, at a cool altitude, 700 m (2000 ft) up, to the east of Soledad in the Salinas Valley. On the lower slopes here Chalone produces a potent but well balanced Chadonnay. Two other heavyweights – Sonoma Cutrer "Les Pierres" and Clos du Bois "Calcaire", both from the cool Sonoma valley, north of San Francisco – also prove that a potent wine of 13° + needn't necessarily be unbalanced.*

grape variety often does repay keeping with considerable development. More recent vintages appear to have been vinified (or "acidified") to be much firmer, for many have wines of a more pronounced acidity, frequently lemony in character, often obtrusively so where added citric acid tastes separate from the fruit. I wonder if the pendulum here hasn't also swung too far? Where you find a zealous acidity look beneath it when tasting to see how many layers of flavour there are, and whether the lingering finish is just a citric acidity or whether it supports persistent flavour and aroma as well. The "lemon and lime" threatens to become as all embracing as oak in Rioja, and similarly tiresome if it underlies too many of the wines; not only Chardonnay! (As the figures are also on the labels, alcohol/acid comparisons can be made too.)

Having said all that, you will find some wonderful wines. The New South Wales Hunter Valley Chardonnays generally seem broader and softer than those from Victoria and South Australia. Amongst the best Tyrrells Vat 47 is elegant, even, not overblown; Rothbury's is generous, deeply flavoured and minerally; the Rosemount wines are brilliantly "showy" early on, having lots of sweet ripe flavour with oak vanilla to match, but they do appear to tire rapidly. The "Roxburgh" vineyard wine is an attempt to make something that will last and develop – I wish I could believe it. Time will tell. However, Allandale's is a must: a broad, buttery and satisfyingly long wine and the Lake's Folly Chardonnay is one of Australia's finest: full and concentrated, but elegantly defined by oak and acidity with a delicious aromatic interest and aftertaste.

From Victoria, Tisdall's Mount Helen has received lots of critical acclaim. It is a vigorous, quality wine and certainly distinctive, but I have yet to come to terms with its oak and limes bouquet and austere, faintly resinous flavour. Mount Mary, from the cool Yarra Valley is really exciting. A beautifully integrated balance of fruit, acid and aromas where oak is a condiment, not an ingredient.

The South Australian Chardonnays seem to me to be the most successful as a group. They are often a blend of grapes from Barossa, Clare and Coonawarra. Orlando's is marvellous value; full, silky and subtly oaky, with an unobtrusive acidity. Wynns Coonawarra Chardonnay is round, creamy and complex; Petaluma's all elegance and refinement, real class. Penfold's is big, concentrated and lingering, buttery but nicely defined. From Western Australia try the excellent Moss Wood, and Houghton.

Heemskirk from Tasmania is hard and angular when young, Te Mata Estate's 86 Elston Chardonnay from New Zealand is a whopping 13.8° with a severe acidity too, intense and impressive on the attack, exhausting on the finish; often a winner in blind tastings, but not an easy wine to drink. Easier, more elegant and aromatic wines from New Zealand are those of Babich, San Marino, Nobilo and Matawhero in particular; all best within a couple of years.

A curious aspect of some New Zealand and Australian Chardonnays is that at only two or three years old, even when their acidity remains high, the taste of the wine can sometimes seem "old", with vegetally mature flavours, flat aromas and a short finish. An anomalous combination of a tired personality in a youthful constitution.

(**Above**) *Adelaide Hills, South Australia – the location of Petaluma winery. Unlike most European wines, the grapes for many Australian and Californian wines do not necessarily all come from close to the winery. In such cases the wines are sold under the brand name alone, (usually that of the winery) rather than the brand name plus place name.*

RIESLING

As a noble grape, Riesling never receives the acclaim that Chardonnay does, yet it is probably even more of an aristocrat and certainly much wider ranging in the styles of wine it makes. Part of the reason behind this must be that it is best known for its sweeter offerings, be they medium dry or almost liqueur like, not so much wines to drink with food, but to sip before or after a meal. They are perhaps additionally unfashionable at present because of the sugar association. But there are also bone dry Rieslings that are every bit as racy as the finest Chardonnays, albeit in a very different style and much more limited quantity. Although "dry" wines, ("trocken" or "halbtrocken") are becoming more popular and being made in greater quantity in Germany, Alsace is where the majority of great dry Rieslings are made.

Two features characterize a good Riesling: a lively to crisp acidity and a unique "oily", "petrolly" bouquet which develops with even a little maturity. This smell is there, amongst others, on all its wines, sweet or dry. In young wines it may only be detectable as a fleeting impression as the wine settles after being swirled; in mature wines it is heady, penetrating and persistent. An Alsace Riesling of two to three years age or more will provide a clear example of this. Like the blackcurrant of Cabernet this is an unmistakable, and essential, clue to Riesling around the world.

Alsace Riesling is always very austere to begin with, particularly next to the more opulent Gewürztraminer and Pinot Gris. It will seem lean and hard when young, but given time to mature (and good ones need eight to ten years) the wines gain the "goût de pétrole" bouquet as the Alsatians call it, sometimes with a hint of honey. Their texture mellows whilst never entirely losing the underlying steely core; and they always remain bone dry, direct and pure. Unripe years may develop a fine bouquet but generally remain mean to taste (1977); but in ripe years such as 1976, 1983 and 1985, Alsace Rieslings like Trimbach's "Clos St Hune", Ostertag's "Muenchberg" and Domaine Weinbach's "Clos St Catherine" are wines which give the palate a particularly harmonious and delicate, yet intense form of gratification when mature.

A few German producers are turning to making absolutely dry Rieslings. Schlossgut Diel in the Nahe is one of these; their trocken wines are a little lighter than the Alsace Rieslings, but they are similarly austere, with great finesse and outstanding length.

Wherever Riesling is vinified elsewhere in the world it almost always has a degree of sweetness, varying from off dry to the intensely sweet Beerenauslese and Trockenbeerenauslese style wines.

Few would disagree that the cream of Rieslings, right across the sweetness spectrum, come from the grape's home, Germany. And the degree of sweetness (largely, although not entirely, based on the ripeness of the grape) is so central to the style of German wines that their classification system is based on the ripeness of the grapes when picked. It is easy to think of the classification system also being an official "quality hierarchy", although this is so only to a very limited degree, the sweetness degree. Sweetest is by no means always "best"!

Roughly speaking, the further north and west you are in German winemaking areas the lighter the wines will be for a given "prädikat" (qv) level, and the more acidity they will have, basically because of less sun-

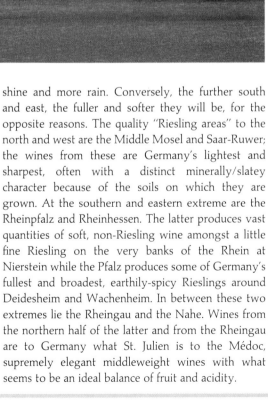

The best way to acquaint yourself with the German Riesling range would be to compare (in this order) a Rheingau Kabinett, Spätlese and Auslese from the same year and property (1985 or 1983 will do nicely). First compare with each other to see the increasing weight and sweetness; and then with a similar line up from the Mosel-Saar-Ruwer and the Rheinpfalz. The Mosel wines will tend to be lighter and crisper for a given prädikat, the Pfalz wines fuller, richer and softer. On some of the Auslese wines you might be able to smell the musk and spice of botrytis, and see how much additional interest this gives to both nose and palate. (Auslese or Beerenauslese wines from 1976, still widely available, would guarantee you a good example.)

(**Below**) *Characteristic* schist *and slate soil in the Central Mosel. Its virtues are that it provides rapid drainage, so minimizing erosion on the precipitous slopes, and it retains the sun's warmth for long after it has set, so helping the grapes to continue ripening.*

shine and more rain. Conversely, the further south and east, the fuller and softer they will be, for the opposite reasons. The quality "Riesling areas" to the north and west are the Middle Mosel and Saar-Ruwer; the wines from these are Germany's lightest and sharpest, often with a distinct minerally/slatey character because of the soils on which they are grown. At the southern and eastern extreme are the Rheinpfalz and Rheinhessen. The latter produces vast quantities of soft, non-Riesling wine amongst a little fine Riesling on the very banks of the Rhein at Nierstein while the Pfalz produces some of Germany's fullest and broadest, earthily-spicy Rieslings around Deidesheim and Wachenheim. In between these two extremes lie the Rheingau and the Nahe. Wines from the northern half of the latter and from the Rheingau are to Germany what St. Julien is to the Médoc, supremely elegant middleweight wines with what seems to be an ideal balance of fruit and acidity.

(**Right**) *Possibly Germany's greatest wine estate. The State Domain at Schlossböckelheim in the Nahe. Just below the winery is the "Hermannsberg" vineyard and behind it the hill of the "Kupfergrube", the old English and Irish owned copper mine, first planted with vines in 1902. Both of these vineyards produce racy, complex Rieslings – exemplary German wine.*

Beerenauslese and Trockenbeerenauslese are Germany's treasures; not only intensely sweet but usually with the additional interest of botrytis. Eiswein is a wine not affected by botrytis, its point is an exceptional concentration of suger and acidity; and for this reason, in spite of its sweetness, I find it the least interesting of Germany's very sweet rarities. The impact on the palate of any of these is often preceded by an equally impressive impact on the purse!

The things to look for in German Rieslings are not a dramatic complexity, richness of flavour or raciness, although the very finest wines may have all of these attributes, instead look for a delicate balance between fruit, sweetness and acidity. The point of these wines when mature is a grace and harmony that no other grape can match, and a glassy-smooth purity of texture which is all the more easy to appreciate because they are wines to sip without food, low in alcohol and easy on the palate. From dry to sweet they are understated, often underestimated, delights.

For comparisons, choose from the top estates where possible: Von Schubert (Maximin Grünhäuser) in the Ruwer, Egon Müller in the Saar; Fritz Haag, Ernst Loosen, J. J. Prüm, or Deinhard in the Middle Mosel. Alternatively the Friedrich-Wilhelm-Gymnasium or Bishöflisches Priesterseminar for all of these

areas. The State Domains (black eagle on the label) are all reliable, but the Nahe one at Schlossböckelheim is outstanding. In the Rheingau there are numerous excellent estates; the State Domain again, Schloss Groenesteyn, Schloss Rheinhartshausen and Schloss Johannisberg to name but a few individually. Look for Anton Balbach in the Rheinhessen; Bürklin-Wolf, Von Buhl and Bassermann Jordan in the Rheinpfalz.

One might be forgiven for thinking Riesling was also important in Germany's southern neighbour Austria, but it accounts for only a very small proportion of wine, mainly from the Wachau region. The sweetest Austrian wines are more commonly from Gewürztraminer and Müller-Thurgau.

Whereas the average German wine will probably be only about 10° of alcohol, and the sweetest perhaps only 6°; the average Californian Riesling, best from the cooler areas of Sonoma and Alexander

Valley, will be 11/12°, off- to medium-dry and with a tendency to softness. They also make late harvest and selected late harvest wines, similar in sweetness to Beerenauslese and Trockenbeerenauslese, where the principal interest seems to be in sweetness and unctuosity, often supported by a distinctly citric acidity. Among the good wines are those of Phelps; Château St. Jean in Sonoma, Mondavi in the Napa; and ZD and Firestone, both made with grapes from the cooler Santa Barbara area. In Oregon's Willamette Valley the grape struggles to ripen, yielding wines that are generally medium-dry, tight, minerally and overall crisper than those from California (Tualatin is particularly good).

Riesling in South Africa seems to lack "cut"; the lesser Paarl Riesling is much more reliable and produces good quality, clean and lively dry wines, if without much personality.

Australian Rhine Riesling is best from the cooler

regions of South Australia, West Australia and Victoria. Except for a few, most peak at two or three years which doesn't give their bouquet much time to develop. The majority are dryish; the less interesting, if very quaffable, wines are a kind of fruity wash, smelling of sherbet and enlivened by carbon dioxide and citric acid, the latter giving them the lemon and lime juice flavour, a taste which marks even the best to some extent.

Among the better wines from South Australia, Hill Smith is an attractive honey and lemon wine, Penfolds Green Ribbon a good middle of the road example and Orlando a fuller, finer style. Petaluma is excellent, a complex, full flavoured dry-spätlese type, very clearly Riesling. Wynns Coonawarra is also a fuller, well balanced wine. From Western Australia try Vasse Felix and especially Leeuwin whose Riesling has depth, drive and length as well as that penetrating petrolly nose. Château Tahbilk makes an interesting, vigorous wine from the Goulburn Valley in Victoria, and Delatite produce a wine that is very pure, fruity and fine if not so very Riesling. New Zealand examples I have tried have been light, floral and pleasant medium-dry wines, but I have not tasted many.

(**Inset left**) *Leeuwin estate in the Margaret River region of Western Australia. It makes, amongst others, an excellent Riesling.*
(**Left**) *Barossa Valley, South Australia. One of Australia's first planted and best known winemaking areas, settled by German immigrants in the mid nineteenth century and now the base for numerous wine names such as Penfolds, Wolf Blass, Seppelt, Yalumba, etc. Here, 500 m (1500 ft) up in the Barossa Range, Orlando's Steingarten Vineyard's cool climate grapes yield an especially refined Riesling.*

SEMILLON

Good dry Semillon comes principally from the Graves region of Bordeaux and from Australia and New Zealand. In its purest form, unblended from the Hunter Valley in Eastern Australia, it is born very plain, with little aroma, a hard, unyielding, almost glassy texture without being particularly acidic, and a flavour that is mean and lemony. But at 10 to 20 years it develops into a beauty of great personality. The bouquet takes on a honeyed, nutty character with the lanolin tone that is so typical of mature Semillon, and the palate, whilst bone dry, becomes rich, silky in texture, mouthfillingly complex. These Hunter wines also seem to have a subtle vanilla flavour and a more distinct minerally, volcanic character as well. Fine examples are the wines of Lindemans, Rothbury Estate (Brokenback Vineyard in particular), Robson, Brokenwood and, more early to mature, MacWilliams Mount Pleasant wines. The latter are called "Riesling", for Semillon from the Hunter is often known, confusingly, as Hunter Valley Riesling.

Quite a different style of Semillon, more precocious and attractively fruity, is made two thousand miles away in Western Australia. Moss Wood and Redgate are two wineries from the Margaret River area producing a quite delicious combination of the softly ripe and really refined. Cape Mentelle is another, blending Sauvignon and Chenin; the Sauvignon dominates on

Lindemans (right) with winemaker Jerry Sissingh, and Rothbury Estate (far right) are wineries in Australia's Hunter Valley, New South Wales – source of Australia's finest Semillon wines. These can age beautifully. A 1965 Lindemans white Burgundy (as it was called then) which I drank in 1985, had all the honey and lanolin character on the nose and the silky rich complexity on the palate that one expects of really great, old white Graves.

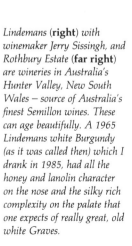

the nose, but this is a supple, gracious, beautifully crafted wine. These may make wonderful old bottles as well, as yet they haven't had the chance to try.

Semillon is sometimes blended with Chardonnay in Australia (Penfolds Chardonnay-Semillon or Semillon-Chardonnay, for example) which makes the wines accessible sooner, the Chardonnay's buttery character combining with the Semillon "lanolin" on the nose, and giving the wine a softer, more flavoury centre.

New Zealand's "pure" Semillons are a curious hybrid. Their clear cut gooseberry-smoky aroma is a Sauvignon masquerade, but on the palate they have more of Semillon's watery purity, certainly none of Sauvignon's acid cut and vibrant fruit. You can sometimes catch a telltale whiff of lanolin after agitating the glass. Good wines of this type come from Villa Maria, Delegats, Babich and Vidal.

The great white Graves wines from Bordeaux are almost always a blend of Semillon and Sauvignon. Laville Haut Brion contains 60 per cent Semillon and 40 per cent Sauvignon, whereas Haut Brion Blanc is nearer 50/50. Haut Brion, owners of Laville since 1983 have retained its previous grape proportions, but increased its proportion of new wood, maybe for the better. Like the Hunter Valley Semillons, they are lean and lemony when young, and similarly the best Graves need 10 years or more to develop. Laville Haut Brion is the archetypal heavyweight example, its best vintages only begin to develop that intriguing waxy richness at 20 years or more. But there are desperately few of these superb yet unfashionable bottles, and the best are expensive. Two new stars on the horizon however *are* cheaper, *are* 100 per cent

(**Opposite top**) *Semillon, ripe to the point of softness; in Bordeaux it is the principle variety used in making Sauternes as well as most of the region's best dry white wines.*
(**Above right and left**) *The Semillon harvest being sorted to exclude any rotten grapes or unripe bunches prior to pressing at Laville Haut Brion in Bordeaux.*

Semillon and, vinified and aged in new oak, look like being very good indeed: Domaine Benoit and Château Constantin. Both show how well Semillon combines with oak and both are made by Peter Vinding Diers, a winemaker much influenced by Australian techniques! The "Y" of Château d'Yquem and the "R" of Château Rieussec are Semillon dominated, dry-ish wines made by these two Sauternes châteaux with the grapes that have insufficient noble rot for the sweet wine. They are hefty, sometimes shapeless curiosities.

Semillon is perhaps better known for its sweet white wines from nobly rotten grapes in the Sauternes region of Bordeaux. Here it is normally blended with Sauvignon Blanc (and possibly a little Muscadelle) to give the wine a bit more backbone, freshness and aroma. A standard blend is 80 per cent Semillon/ 20 per cent Sauvignon Blanc. Guiraud, however, has a remarkable 45 per cent Sauvignon, Filhot 32 per cent Sauvignon and Doisy-Daëne is unique in being made from 100 per cent Semillon. But the style of the wines would seem to be more influenced by the winemaking (and possibly the location) than by the grape mix: Filhot, with its one third Sauvignon, deliberately makes a lighter, fresher, early maturing wine; Guiraud on the other hand, with almost half Sauvignon Blanc, is usually a typically rich and concentrated Sauternes; and the carefully made 100 per cent Semillon Doisy-Daëne lacks for nothing in freshness and elegance of balance.

As a sweet white wine Sauternes is attractive to drink almost from the moment it is bottled, but even lesser vintages improve considerably with five years or so in bottle to allow the sugar and acidity to marry, and the botrytis character to develop. Top wines from great years (those two or three vintages per decade with ample and evenly distributed botrytis) such as 1971, 1975, 1976, 1983, 1986 and 1988, need ten years or more to show at their best. Even when noble rot obliges, the ideal Sauternes balance is not easy to achieve. Balance between sweetness and alcohol is just as crucial as the more obvious balance between sweetness and acidity. Too much alcohol and inadequate sweetness make the wine seem hot and hard; insufficient alcohol and/or too much sugar make the wines taste too soft and cloying. Too *much* acidity is rarely a problem.

Barsacs are generally considered to be lighter, fresher, more "appley" in bouquet than Sauternes proper, but with mature wines the distinction is about as easy to make as that between a St Julien and a Margaux or a St Julien and a Pauillac. D'Yquem apart, amongst the most reliable wines at present are Climens, Guiraud, Raymond Lafon, Doisy-Daëne, Bastor-Lamontagne, and, since 1983, Lafaurie-Peyraguey and Rieussec.

Wines from the lesser, neighbouring appellations of Cérons, Loupiac and St Croix-du-Mont, and also from Monbazillac in Bergerac, are similar in style to Sauternes, but usually lighter, less intensely sweet and coarser textured. Nevertheless, the best of them are more than a match for poorly made Sauternes.

Outside France sweet "botrytized" Semillons are rare, but De Bortoli and Lindemans make a very appealing, concentratedly sweet and honeyed wine in New South Wales, Australia; and Australian winemaker Peter Bright produces a similar wine in Portugal for João Pires.

CHENIN BLANC

My feelings about Chenin Blanc are more ambivalent than about any other grape. At the horror end of its spectrum are some of the most sicky(*sic*)-sulphury abominations to be found in a bottle (usually off-dry to medium-sweet wines from the Loire); whilst at the heavenly end are wonderfully racy dry wines and ethereally fine sweet ones, also mainly from the Loire.

Few Chenin wines that are produced outside France can match the quality of the finest French offerings, and none of them have the steely acidity which is the key feature of the French Chenin. In South Africa Chenin Blanc is also known as the Steen; it accounts for 25 per cent of their wine grapes and, as in France, makes every style of white wine from bone dry to intensely sweet. The dry wines are largely very well made and uncomplicated: clean, appley-fragrant to smell and taste, usually with a touch of spritz. "Late

(**Top left**) The "emietteur", (literally fragmenter) at Yquem. After the first and second pressings, the compressed cake of grapes is loaded from the press into this apparatus whose jagged teeth break up and loosen the compacted mass so that it can be effectively pressed further. (**Bottom left**) Nectar must for nectar wine, from the third and final pressing of nobly rotten grapes: the most intense and liquorous juice of all.

suggestion in the dry Anjou wines, to wet-wool or damp straw with a touch of honey in the sweeter versions. The worst remind me of boiled sweets, fermented cheeses and malic, unripe apples. What a catalogue!

The most exciting dry Chenins come from Savennières, a small appellation on the north bank of the Loire southwest of Angers. In these wines one really can seem to smell the flinty soil; and to taste they are taut, bone dry, close grained and racy; impressive, if austere, when young but ageing beautifully. Château de la Bizolière, Château de Chamboureau and Clos de la Bergerie are all excellent. Roches-aux-Moines and Coulée de Serrant are two small appellations within Savennières producing wines that are even more highly wrought and concentrated, Mme Joly's Coulée de Serrant monopoly especially.

South of the river is the extensive appellation of Coteaux du Layon producing medium sweet wines with a wax and wet-wool nose. Jean Baumard's Clos de Ste Catherine is one of the lighter of these but it is always an agreeably fresh and flowery wine. Almost all the sweeter wines (and the dry Vouvrays and Montlouis) seem to have a suggestion of honey in both bouquet and taste, and Quarts de Chaume and Bonnezeaux, two small areas within the Coteaux du Layon, frequently add the complexity of botrytis to this. They are richer, sweeter wines needing years to lose their steely acidity and become harmonious, but rewarding when they do. Try Domaine des Baumards and Château de Fesles.

Vouvray and Montlouis, respectively on the north and south banks of the Loire just east of Tours, make Chenin wines from dry to sweet, and from faintly "pétillant" to proper sparkling. The dry wines are generally less aromatic but fruitier than Savennières; looser, more open textured and with a bouquet smelling more of honey and the faint bitter sweetness of quince. Gaston Huet makes the most searingly acidic of all the Vouvrays when young, needing ten years at least to even begin to yield, but promising wonderful wine for those prepared to wait. Other good producers from Vouvray are Poniatowski and Marc Brédif; and if you ever get a chance to taste one of the Maison Prunier Vouvrays or Anjous, do not miss it. The finest Chenin wine I have had was a 1959 Maison Prunier Vouvray "Les Clos". At nearly 30 years of age it was remarkably fresh to smell, with a fine spun, delicate honeyed flavour and a flawless, almost glassy texture; lacy, ethereal and lingering. That's the heavenly side of Chenin!

harvest" wines tend not to be the intensely sweet wines found under that name in California, they are late harvest in the literal German sense of "spät-lese" meaning late-picked, and they are spätlese in style, usually with excellent fruit. The sweetest and most famous "steen" wine is Edelkeur, a botrytis wine which will stand comparison with any of the world's great sweet wines.

Californian Chenin Blanc is mostly unexceptional wine; bland, off-dry and lacking definition. One of the best is that from Dry Creek, but as a group they are, as yet, hardly worth seeking out. Much the same can be said for Australian Chenin Blanc. The best have an appealing fruit juice character and little else. The New Zealand wines are also a mixed bag, although the climate would seem more promising for the grape. Collard's Dry Chenin is the best I have tasted.

Acidity is the key to Chenin in France. Its wines are not particularly full in body, although they can certainly be concentrated, and its bouquet varies from a waxy, unfruity character often with a smoky

SAUVIGNON BLANC

The name Sauvignon derives via the French "sauvage", meaning wild, from the Latin "silva" a wood. And in its most emphatic form, there is nothing urbane about this grape at all. When young and fresh it has an almost spikily penetrating aroma, variously described as gooseberry or blackcurrant leaf; sometimes also chalky, smoky or flinty in character. With a bit of age this can become more vegetal, musk like or "catty", as in cat's pee, although I have never found the last description very helpful, not on the evidence of my cats anyway. The palate echoes the theme of freshness and greenery for these are wines that taste very much of their smell: crisp, uncomplicated, above all aromatic. Once their pungency has gone, pure, unoaked Sauvignons lose most of their point.

You can find these characteristics in a raw, brash form in basic Sauvignons from Touraine or Haut Poitou, and just as clearly in Sauvignon de St Bris, near Chablis. The classic example though is Sancerre, along with its neighbours of Ménetou-Salon, Reuilly,

(Right) The vineyards, winery and castle of the 19th century Château du Nozet in Pouilly on a May morning. A typical Loire hunting lodge cum country residence on the edge of thick forest, it is fairytale in appearance if not in period. Once visited, scenes like this surface instantly at the scent and savour of the local wine, adding immeasurably to its appeal.

Quincy and Pouilly-Fumé. The latter is often more supple, fragrant and finely textured than Sancerre (try the wines of Château de Tracy, Grebet or Jean Claude Chatelain) a less gross and more refined version of Sauvignon.

Bordeaux's range of this grape is much wider, and the bottom end much less reliable than the Loire product. Even where it is not mixed with other grapes, the warmer climate makes for a wine that is more ivory than greeny-yellow in colour and whose accent is less pronounced, as in the best Entre-Deux-Mers for example. Much cheap white Bordeaux though manages to be flat and tart at once; sweetish and neutral to smell, blandly fruitless, sometimes resinous to taste.

But Bordeaux also boasts some of the most illustrious examples of Sauvignon Blanc. The majority of them are blended with Semillon. Two however are pure Sauvignon: Malartic Lagravière from the Graves region, and Château Margaux's Pavillon Blanc from the Médoc. Although 100 per cent Sauvignon Blanc does not usually improve with age, 1970 and 1955 Malartic tasted at 17 and 32 years old respectively were a lively, refined and complex exception, with the benefit of very little oak. The more oaky Domaine de Chevalier (70 per cent Sauvignon/30 per cent Semillon) also develops beautifully in bottle and Fieuzal (60/40) is making increasingly impressive white

wines. On the subject of maturity I have had an impressive old Chavignol from Francis Cottat in Sancerre, which at fifteen years was still a perfumed Sauvignon, broad, supple and lingering.

Sauvignon Blanc from Bulgaria or northern Italy may be pleasant wines, but their varietal character is at best muted. Much the same goes for the Chilean versions from Torres and Concha y Toro, which are soft, fruity and sweetish. Australia's Sauvignon Blanc and "Fumé Blanc" range from soft, sweet oaky-fruit concoctions that leave one hunting for any vestige of Sauvignon, to attractively grassy and aromatic versions like Middlebrook's understated Sauvignon Blanc, the elegant Fumé Blanc of Enterprise and Taltarni's broad yet delicately fine example. The cooler climate of New Zealand seems better suited to the grape's aromatic personality with increasingly good, full bodied examples from Montana, Selaks, Delegats, Coopers Creek and a deliciously refined Cloudy Bay.

Mondavi's Californian Fumé Blanc is a highly individual expression of the grape; blended with a minute amount of Semillon and aged in oak, it is a beautifully balanced rich, velvety wine with a subtle smoky character which improves for several years in bottle. Dry Creek is another tangy wine, but most Californians are fairly heavy and unctuous examples; a far cry from those brisk, wild Loiresides.

(**Above**) *Domaine de Chevalier in Bordeaux, whose dry white Graves testifies to Sauvignon's ability to age. Though different in style, its quality, and now indeed its price, are on a par with Grand Cru white Burgundy.* (**Opposite**) *The hilltop fortress town of Sancerre and its surrounding vineyards in the Central Loire. Sancerre's white wines have long been the archetypal example of crisp and pungently aromatic Sauvignon Blanc, but New Zealand's Sauvignons are often just as clear cut, if somewhat stronger.*

GEWÜRZTRAMINER

Gewürz means "spice" in German, and spice is certainly one of this grape's most obvious characteristics, especially in wines from Alsace where the most individual Gewürztraminers are made.

The typical constitution of Gewürztraminer is fairly high in alcohol, fairly low in acidity. When the grape is fully ripe its skin has a pinkish tinge and even young wines can have a deep yellow colour. However, the nose and flavour of Gewürztraminer are what make it so distinctive. It has a noticeably perfumed bouquet that has variously been described as reminiscent of lychees, rosewater, violet cachous, guava or Turkish Delight – which certainly covers the fragrance options for most noses. Alsace Gewürztraminers are broad and mouthfilling, almost unctuous in texture, with a dry yet luscious "lychee" taste and a marked spiciness. They are wines which are easy to recognize, perhaps less easy to drink (in quantity anyway) and partner with food, as they can be rather overwhelming. This is particularly so in the "Vendange Tardive" (late harvest) wines of exceptional vintages such as 1976 or 1983. Even when dry these wines are honeyed, powerfully aromatic and often have the added interest and complexity of noble rot. They can be impressive in their flavour concentration, but can just as easily be too heavy; potent wines lacking in acidity, sluggish and clinging on the palate, best sipped rather than drunk. The wines of Hugel and Trimbach are widely available and interesting to compare because the Trimbach wines generally have a higher acidity. Faller Frères (Domaine Weinbach) make polished wines, as do Domaine Ostertag.

There are two other "heavyweight" Alsace wines that can sometimes be confused with Gewürztraminer: Muscat and Pinot Gris (Tokay d'Alsace'). Both may have a "musk" character on the nose (yet another feature of Gewürztraminer too), but they are easier to distinguish on the palate. Good Pinot Gris is firmer, less unctuous and tastes "drier", with none of the lychee flavour; Muscat can often feel similar with a low acidity and an unctuous texture, but it generally tastes fruitier, grapier and lighter, with less breadth, spice and power than Gewürztraminer or Pinot Gris.

German examples, from the warmer areas of the Rheinhessen, Palatinate and Baden, are usually in a "trocken" style, off-dry and fuller than most German wines, and having the characteristic nose and flavour. Those from Austria on the other hand are usually in a decidedly sweet style: Auslese, Beerenauslese or

(**Top right**) A bunch of Gewürztraminer with the ripe grapes showing the distinctly pinky-brown hue that often gives Gewürztraminer must a pinky-orange colour (**below, opposite**), and its wines a deep yellow tinge even when young.

(**Right**) The northern extremity of the Haut Rhin region in Alsace, looking west towards St Hypolite and showing the protected lie of the Haut Rhin vineyards in the lee of the Vosge mountains. This range protects the vines from excessive rain (precipitated on the western slopes) and makes Alsace one of the driest European wine regions at this latitude. It is also one of the warmest. Alsace Gewürztraminer is rarely wanting in alcohol, it is not infrequently wanting in acidity!

Trockenbeerenauslese. They are delicious sweet wines, the first two categories especially, although at this level of sweetness the wines smell of honey and barley sugar; with only an oily texture and barely perceptible spice to say they are Gewürztraminer at all. With their relatively low acidity these are best drunk young and fresh, before they taste and smell of marmalade and toffee!

Gewürztraminers from the South Tyrol in Italy are in a lighter style, soft and musky when young, often acquiring an earthy, vegetal character with any age. Also best drunk young.

The most successful American versions come from Oregon and Washington where they are noticeably lighter, drier and firmer than the Alsace wines but still retaining a distinct Gewürztraminer nose and spicy flavour. Australia has found it more difficult to make distinctive Gewürztraminers so far, and often blends the grape with Rhine Riesling to make it less bland. A wine like Delatite's from Victoria is a beautifully crafted, fruity wine with an almost Riesling purity. It has just a hint of musk and lychee on the nose, but nothing to reveal that it is Gewürztraminer on the palate. The first time I tasted this wine (in London) I said as much to the lady standing next to me, and got a frank and spicy earful in return — before she revealed she was the winemaker!

New Zealand is the non-French success story for this grape. The wines' bouquets are rarely as pronounced as those of Alsace but they have all the typical dry-yet-luscious spiced lychee flavour on the palate. The best wines are made with grapes from the North Island Gisborne area and the dry ones are better than the sweeter versions. Coopers Creek, Villa Maria and Matawhero are all excellent.

(**Top left**) *Pierre Trimbach, dwarfed by the enormous oak vats used both for fermenting and ageing Trimbach's Alsace wines. These vats develop a substantial tartrate deposit on the inside, often several centimetres thick which needs hammering off every three or four years.*

(**Below**) *The characteristic pinkish-orange colour of Gewürztraminer must, in this case from ripe grapes at Coopers Creek, New Zealand. New Zealand is the source of some of the best non-European Gewürztraminer wines.*

MUSCAT

The smell of Muscat grapes is so distinctive and instantly recognizable, that it is the only wine grape which doesn't have wine buffs or wine writers desperately searching for analogous smells to assist in identifying it. Muscat smells of Muscat (perhaps of Philadelphus, Syringa, "Mock Orange" if you press me). This remarkable perfume is also the reason why most Muscat wines are made sweet. The Muscat smell is chemically linked to the grape's sugars and if these are all transformed into alcohol the fragrance is lost at the same time. Stop the fermentation before all the sugar is turned to alcohol and you keep the perfume with the sweetness. The combination is usually irresistible as early winemakers must quickly have discovered. And chemist or not, experience bears this out, dry Muscats have little of the distinctive grapey bouquet of the sweet wines; and if they do at all it is nothing like as pronounced. Muscat d'Alsace is the best known of the dry wines, Brown Bros make a good Dry Muscat Blanc in Australia, João Pires a good off-dry wine in Portugal; and delicate, fragrant rarities are made under the names Rosenmuskateller and Goldenmuskateller in Italy's Alto-Adige.

Unashamedly sweet wines, however, are what Muscat is really about. The most easily available is the Italian sparkling wine Asti Spumante or Moscato d'Asti, ridiculously derided for its sweetness but a deliciously light, frothy wine. Grown much more popular (and much more expensive) recently is Muscat de Beaumes de Venise from the Côtes du Rhône in France, an intensely sweet but very fragrant wine. This is one of a number of French "Vin Doux Naturel", misleadingly named, for they are in fact fortified wines with 15°–16° of actual alcohol (not 21.5° as is often stated, the additional 6° or so is still in the wine as unfermented sugar). Muscat de Frontignan from the southwest of France is another of these, as is Muscat de Rivesaltes from the same region, although the Frontignan is much the finer, similar in quality to a good Beaumes de Venise or Samos "nectar", a Muscat from the Greek island of that name.

Spanish and Portuguese Muscats are called Moscatels and are made from the less good quality Muscat of Alexandria grape which produces a coarser, less fragrant wine. (All the wines in the previous paragraph, with the exception of the Rivesaltes, are made from the finer Muscat à Petit Grains, also known as the Muscat de Frontignan.) This shows in the Spanish

Moscatel de Valencia: soft and raisiny, sticky unless well chilled; and in the Portuguese Moscatel de Setúbal which has a coarse earthiness under its concentrated sweetness. Wines with a blend of Alexandrian Muscat and other grapes are Spanish Malaga (with Pedro Ximenez – known as PX), and Banyuls and Maury from the eastern Pyrenees region of France (both with white Grenache). Grand Cru Banyuls can be very good at 10 to 15 years with up to 20° of alcohol, off-dry to sweet in flavour and with a noticeable *rancio*.

Candidates for the world's greatest sweet Muscats must be the Australian Liqueur Muscats made from the Frontignan variety and with about 18° alcohol. The best come from Rutherglen in northeast Victoria. These are fabulously concentrated, intensely sweet but superbly balanced wines with great complexity and length; a dessert by themselves. Any of these liqueur wines from Morris, Stanton and Killeen, Baileys or Chambers will be memorable. My favourite is the Chambers Rosewood Vineyards "Special", an exceptionally graceful wine for one so sweet; and more finely balanced than their "Old" liqueur Muscat, in theory a superior wine, but a case of more not necessarily being better.

See also Tokay Muskatolyos (page 75).

MUSCADET

This grape is also known as the Melon de Bourgogne from its Burgundian origins; it has nothing to do with Mus*cat*. Muscadet wine comes from the Atlantic end of the Loire. It is a gulping white, with few exceptions pale in colour and pale in character. Its principal feature is a fresh and simple neutrality on nose and palate. It is crisp and dry but lacking any noticeable aromatic character or development on the palate. As a Loire wine, acidity is relatively high, but it is more a "bone-dry" wine than an acid one. If it smells of anything much it tends towards a faint wet-wool, sometimes "mealy" character; with good "sur lie" wines (bottled straight off their lees) having a hint of yeastiness and spritz. A few Muscadets will keep and improve in bottle, the vast majority will not.

VIOGNIER

An *uva rara* even for professionals, effectively limited to the northern Rhône Valley where it may be part of Côte Rôtie's make up but where it is principally used to make Condrieu and Château Grillet. Viognier is usually deep yellow in colour, occasionally with a rosé tinge, and has a heady bouquet that is fragrant, peachy, occasionally musky as well. Its impressions on the palate are of high alcohol, moderate acidity and a mouthfilling silky texture. The wine is vinified dry, but has so much alcohol (13° plus) it has a barely dry, luscious flavour; broad, perfumed and rich, slow to develop on the palate, warm and spicy on the finish, often with a hint of almond kernel bitterness.

(**Left**) *Viognier in the Côte Rôtie, northern Rhône, where the grape grows in amongst the red vines on the paler soil of the Côte Blonde. Up to 20% is permitted, though rarely used, in the red wine. Where a significant proportion is used, it makes for a Côte Rôtie that is paler in colour and more perfumed in bouquet than most Hermitage.*
(**Below**) *Amidst its terraced vineyards right on the edge of the river Rhône, Château Grillet has its own tiny AC within Condrieu and is the most famous Viognier wine, best drunk while it is young and fresh.*

*Monsieur Flandin in his tiny
Rhône cellar where a
nineteenth century cement
press, fibreglass vat and old
barrels make a heady white
Crozes Hermitage from
Marsanne and Roussanne
(russet coloured) grapes.*

MARSANNE AND ROUSSANNE

It makes sense to deal with these two varieties together as you will rarely encounter them apart, but most likely as a blend in the white wines of the northern Rhône. Roussanne is the better quality grape, but its yield is lower and it is also more difficult to grow so much more Marsanne is planted. The whites of St Joseph and Crozes-Hermitage are almost exclusively Marsanne, as is the sparkling St-Péray. Hermitage is more commonly a 50/50 blend, and Château de Beaucastel's white Châteauneuf-du-Pape is 80 per cent Roussanne.

Both grapes make full bodied wine with lowish acidity. Young Marsanne dominated wines have an "apple and pear" nose and a fairly heavy, straightforward fruity flavour to match (try the white Crozes of Jaboulet, Desmeure, Tardy & Ange). Rousanne in the blend makes for a much more interesting wines such as white Hermitage, smelling of nuts, meal and hay when young and developing an oily weight with age. These wines also have a spicier flavour, often marked by an almond or walnut bitterness. Jaboulet's Chevalier de Sterimberg is now deliberately vinified to make "fresher", younger drinking style of Hermitage; Grippat's white Hermitage is perhaps the most elegant and stylish of them all, Chapoutier's Chante Alouette and Chave's wines are in the headier, heavier old fashioned style, needing and repaying keeping for up to ten years and more.

A little Marsanne is vinified in Australia; Mitchelton's wine from central Victoria is the best I have tried; full bodied, vigorous and lightly oaky. Only in alcohol does it resemble the French version.

ADDITIONAL WHITE GRAPE VARIETIES

PINOT BLANC
A shadowy grape making soft, dry, bland wines. Characteristics unclear apart from low acidity and rather plain fruit without much depth. Best (= heaviest?) from Alsace.

MÜLLER-THURGAU
Uncertain parentage: either Riesling × Riesling, or Riesling × Sylvaner. Germany's most widely planted variety (about 25 per cent), mainly in the Rheinhessen, Rheinpfalz and Baden, and principal constituent of Liebfraumilch. From Germany the wines are light, soft and blandly fruity with a faintly "muscatty" nose when young; any bottle age produces something more grassy and vegetal. Better cut wines, agreeably fresh, come from England and New Zealand.

SEYVAL BLANC AND SCHÖNBURGER
Apart from Müller-Thurgau, the principal grapes for English wine. Both somewhat fuller in body than the former, with Schönburger also richer and having a bit more scent on the nose and spice on the palate.

SCHEUREBE
Scheurebe makes excellent German wines from Auslese upwards. It has both plenty of acidity and depth of flavour, if not Riesling's elegant purity. It never gets Riesling's oily nose in maturity either, but has instead a distinctive aroma of grapefruit skin/zest, sometimes blackcurrant leaf. The grape makes excellent value Beerenauslese.

KERNER
Another German grape which makes excellent sweet wines with lots of lemony acidity and barley sugar sweetness. As with Scheurebe there is no Riesling "oil" on the mature wines, nor the latter's race and length; and as distinct from Scheurebe it doesn't have the individual grapefruit-skin or blackcurrant leaf nose. Similarly good quality though.

SYLVANER
Generally low in flavour, high in acidity, but crispness apart rather devoid of personality. A slight earthiness in German wines from the Rheinhessen and Rheinpfalz; a little more fullness and breadth in the dry wines from Alsace.

RIESLING – LASKI-, OLASZ-, WELSCH-, GREY-, -ITALICO, PAARL- ETC.

The Riesling pretender. Planted worldwide and producing wines with none of the Rhine Riesling class whatsoever. In general, these are soft medium-dry wines that are quaffable, little more. Vast quantities are sold on the basis of lowest common denominator appeal, that denominator being blandness. For many of us the first and entirely forgettable introduction to wine.

ALIGOTÉ

Mostly from Burgundy and mostly plain and flat in character, although drinkable because of an attractively lively acidity. The best have an appley nose, ripe fruit and a certain buttery breadth to them. Enough to fool one into confusing them with lesser Chardonnays. For proof of which, try those of Tabit (from St. Bris near Chablis), Capron-Manieux and Daniel Rion. As aligotés they will surprise you.

GRÜNER VELTLINER

Austria's own speciality. Greeny yellow in colour; dry and grapey with a delicate spritz and a very distinct peppery spice on the palate and often on the nose too. At its bubbly, cool and barely fermented best, straight from the cask as draught wine called Heuriger, named after the Viennese inns in which the latest vintage is to be found in barrel.

SZÜRKEBARAT

Pinot Gris from Hungary, where the tastiest wines are broad, dry, minerally examples from Mount Badacsony on Lake Balaton. Not quite as exciting and individual as Keknyelü.

KEKNYELÜ

You are unlikely to find this with any ease outside Hungary, but it is such a distinctive, characterful wine that it is worth trying if ever you come across it. One of those wines that really does taste of the dark volcanic-ash soil in which the grapes are grown on the slopes of Mount Badacsony. Broad and full; dry, fiery and minerally in flavour.

HARSLEVELÜ

Most attractive, by itself, as Debroi Harslevelü; a rich, medium-dry wine with a fragrant, honeyed nose and a spicy, spirited flavour from Hungary's northern Massif. Best known for being the partner to Furmint in the production of Tokay.

FURMINT

At its most famous and finest as the principal grape in Hungary's *Tokay* (50–60 per cent). All Tokays, whether dry or sweet are characterized by a deep gold to amber colour, a slightly oxydized bouquet of burnt caramel or burnt orange, and a flavour which has a distinct fiery, volcanic spice, supported by a penetrating acidity. The various Tokay styles are:

Tokay Szamorodni Meaning literally "as it comes". Wine made from unselected grapes which may turn out dry (*szaraz*) or sweet (*edes*) according to the weather pattern and ripeness of the grapes.

Tokay Aszu A wine of varying degrees of sweetness according to the proportion of *aszu* (nobly rotten grapes) used. These grapes are crushed to a paste in 35 litre hods (*puttonyos*, "putts" for short), before being added to 140 litre barrels of standard dry wine which is then left to referment very slowly for a number of years. The more puttonyos of aszu added per barrel, the sweeter the wine will be: "6" is sweetest.

Tokay Muskatolyos Aszu As above, but made principally from Muscat grapes. A similar but even richer and sweeter style for a given number of "putts".

Tokay Aszu Essencia The rarest available wine, made exclusively from aszu grapes. When I have been able to try them together I have preferred the "six putts" to the Essencia. The latter is sweeter, but also thicker, less harmonious and less refined.

SAVAGNIN

A grape unique to the Jura in northeast France, used for the long lived *Vins Jaunes*, of which Château-Chalon is the most famous. As with all long lived wines the Savagnin has a piercingly high acidity when young, and it is "young" for at least two decades. After a slow fermentation the dry wine is put into casks and left for a minimum of six years without being topped up. It is prevented from oxydizing by a flor yeast like that on Sherry except that this is black, not white.

The wines are characterized by a pungent, nutty aroma, and by an absolutely bone dry, aromatic lemon and walnut flavour of an exceptional austerity. They are not fortified like sherry, are usually only about 13°–14° and are much more severely dry than dry Sherry. After a couple of decades they start to soften and develop a honey and rancio character on the nose, and a blend of lemony youth and caressing mellow complexity on the palate. Henri Maire's Château-Chalon softens a little earlier; Jean Bourdy's and Château d'Arlay's wines need longer but are wonderful rarities given time.

RED WINEMAKING

(**Right**) *Grapes are picked in whole bunches if the picking is done by hand, as here; but mechanical pickers, which are increasingly common, vibrate the vine trunk and literally shake the individual grapes off the stems.*

(**Below**) *A "stemmer-crusher" machine. The whole bunches are fed into the cylindrical sieve. As this rotates the grapes are stripped and pass through the holes into the milled rollers below which release the juice, while the stems are blown out at the far end.*

PICKING

Just as with white, the quality of red wine will only be as good as the grapes that are used to make it, and although the moment when the grapes are picked is not as crucial as for white wines it will nevertheless affect their style. Grapes picked early have less sugar, more acid, less colour and less ripe tannin; their style will be lighter, fresher and perhaps paler. In a cold year they will be thinner and greener. Grapes picked late will yield richer wines with more alcohol, colour and tannin. The danger of picking too late and too ripe is that the wines will lack acidity and may taste "jammy".

CRUSHING

The grapes are "crushed" as soon as they are harvested, meaning, as with white grapes, that their skins are broken to release the juice. The more gentle this is the better. Any harsh treatment of the skins will result in harsh tannin. At this stage the grapes may be separated entirely from their stems, or a proportion of the stems retained to give more tannin where the grapes don't contain enough.

Maceration is what accounts for the difference between red and white wines. This is the steeping of the grape's skins, pips and possibly stems in the fermenting must where the alcohol acts as a solvent and extracts their colour, tannin and aromatic elements. Red wines are fermented with their skins, white wines are not.

FERMENTATION

In order to promote the extraction of colour and tannin, red wines are fermented much warmer than whites, usually between 25° and 30°C (77° and 86°F). Above 30° (86°F) there is a danger of the fermentation "sticking" as it is too hot for the yeast, or the wines will begin to taste "cooked". Cold fermentation, below 20°C (68°F), is possible but unusual. As tannin is an antioxydant red wines are less susceptible to oxydation so fermentation in open vats is quite possible, if increasingly rare.

Chaptalization If the winemaker decides his wine will need slightly more alcohol to improve its balance, he will add sugar early on in the fermentation process.

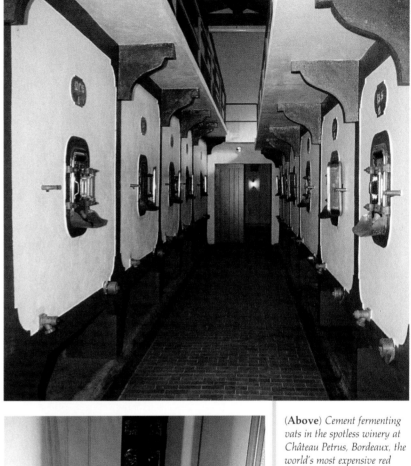

(Above) Cement fermenting vats in the spotless winery at Château Petrus, Bordeaux, the world's most expensive red wine. You don't have to have stainless steel to make good wine!

(Far left) Taking the temperature of the must. If it is too cold it will need warming before it can ferment.

(Left) Before fermentation must is also analyzed for its sugar level. If this is inadequate the rarely seen bags of sugar will be used for chaptalization.

Vatting time How long the winemaker keeps his wine in contact with the grape skins depends on the grapes he is vinifying and the style of wine he seeks to make. "Noble" red grapes (eg Cabernet, Pinot, Syrah, Nebbiolo) are noble because their skins are rich in good quality tannins and aromas. These are the varieties that benefit from long maceration. "Common" varietals (Cinsaut, Malbec for example) are so called because the tannin and aroma constituents of their skins are less fine, so that prolonged skin contact only extracts coarse elements: green, vegetal, bitter, hard.

Brief maceration, running the must off the skins after three or four days will produce soft, supple wines for drinking young. Although containing very little tannin they will have plenty of colour, as most of the colour is extracted early on in the fermentation, well before the tannin. Rosé wines usually have less than 24 hours contact before the must is run off and they finish fermenting in the same way as white wines. Moderately tannic, medium term wines will have six to eight days vatting, Burgundy for example; and tannic wines for long keeping will be in contact with the skins from 10 to 20 days, sometimes longer.

(**Top right**) *Pumping over: a regular operation which submerges the cap and prevents it spoiling, promotes the extraction of colour and tannin, and ensures the even fermentation in the vat by thoroughly mixing the must.*
(**Centre right**) *A close up of the "cap", the floating mass of skins and pips that needs to be punched down regularly, or submerged by "pumping over" with the liquid from the bottom of the vat.*
(**Below right**) *Must and skins arriving in the vat, pumped straight from the stemmer crusher.*
(**Opposite, top left**) *A modern "bladder press". A rubber bag is very slowly inflated, pressing the saturated skins against the perforated walls very gently, thus avoiding any coarse tannin extraction.*
(**Opposite, top right**) *Press wine. The first press (left) may be used to bolster the free-run wine with extra colour, tannin and flavour; the second press (right) is just too coarse grained and astringent . . . even to look at!*

Pressing After the "free run" (first) wine has been run off, the remaining mass of skins and pips is pressed to obtain a further 10–15 per cent of liquid. Pressed wine has more of everything (colour, tannin, flavour) except acidity, and may eventually be used to bolster the free run wine. Only the first fraction is used as the final extract is just too bitter and astringent.

Malolactic fermentation After the alcoholic fermentation has finished, the malolactic fermentation is usually sought for tannic red wines. Here the sourer malic acid is converted into the softer lactic acid by bacteria (as opposed to yeast in the alcoholic fermentation).

Ageing Depending on their quality and constitution, red wines will be aged in wooden barrels, usually oak, of varying sizes, for anywhere between six and 24 months.

Racking and fining While the wine is maturing in wood, solid particles left over from fermentation slowly settle, and every now and again the wines are decanted off this sediment ("racked") into clean barrels. Before bottling wines may be "fined", and possibly filtered, in order to render them stable and brilliant. Fining removes any suspended matter in the wine which could mar its clarity. A variety of agents are used for this, the most famous of which is egg white. The principle is exactly the same as that used in the kitchen to clarify consommé soup.

(**Above**) *Racking: periodic decanting of a wine off any sediment and into clean barrels.*
(**Left**) *Fining: using beaten egg white; this is well mixed into the wine, then, as it settles, it draws with it (physically and electrochemically) any suspended matter that hasn't already settled.*

CABERNET SAUVIGNON

Cabernet Sauvignon must be the world's most famous grape variety. Like Chanel No 5, you probably know the name even if you don't know the product. As with Chardonnay for white wine, Cabernet has become a synonym for quality red from producers the world over; and for the same reasons: it travels and adapts well to many different soils and climates. Unlike pure Chardonnay's more muted personality however, Cabernet's distinctive "blackcurrant" aroma is a re-curring motif, although in different guises, almost wherever it grows and whatever the local style.

Mention Cabernet Sauvignon and almost anyone with even a slight knowledge of wine will instantly think of Claret. Yet Claret, Cabernet's most well known product, doesn't advertize the Cabernet connection at all. It has always been a blended wine, a blend of different grape varieties that is. Its name derives from the French "clairet" meaning light in colour, a description of early Bordeaux made from whatever grapes were available, red and white being fermented together to produce a pale rose-coloured wine. Today the laws of many wine producing countries would not permit the majority of clarets to call themselves Cabernet Sauvignon, for most of them contain under 75 per cent of the grape. Even those are limited to the Médoc and Graves areas, the so-called "left bank" of the Gironde Estuary and of the River Garonne. Whilst a few Médocs such as Mouton Rothschild (85 per cent) and Latour (80 per cent) contain a high proportion of Cabernet Sauvignon, the majority make do with 60–70 per cent, the balance being largely made up of Merlot and Cabernet Franc. This "mix" is the result of several factors: historical accident, the suitability of soils for individual varieties, the need to spread the risk of one grape "failing" in any harvest and the demands of a desired style. But Cabernet Sauvignon is so well suited to the gravelly soils of the Graves and Médoc that its character domi-nates even where it is only half to two thirds of a blend.

(**Above right**) *Claret, unlike Burgundy, is made from a blend of grapes; a blend is almost invariably more complete than any of its individual contributory wines, as a tasting such as this one at Leoville Las Cases would show. Here a typical final blend, the Grand Vin, is made up of 65% Cabernet Sauvignon, 17% Merlot, 13% Cabernet Franc and 5% Petit Verdot, reflecting the planting of the vineyard. The exact proportions will vary according to the individual vintages.*
(**Right**) *Château Sénéjac in the central Médoc in Bordeaux, showing the well drained, gravelly soil in which Cabernet Sauvignon thrives. The wine has the characteristic fine earthyness of flavour that seems to come from Cabernet Sauvignon grapes grown on this type of soil.*

The Cabernet Sauvignon grape is small and thick skinned, yielding wine that is dark purple in colour, with plenty of acid and tannin. It is not an alcoholic wine, at least not in Bordeaux. As we shall see, the "blackcurrant" smell comes in many different forms. In Bordeaux, young Cabernet smells of raw blackcurrants (rather than cassis); it has something of the aromatic freshness of Sauvignon Blanc, to which it is related, and often has a faint earthy quality as well (freshly moistened soil, or a garden after rain). Cabernet here also often smells of cedar wood, sometimes likened to "cigar-box" wood, but this tends to be when it is more mature, and derives as much from contact with new oak as from the grape itself.

For a Bordeaux Cabernet smell uninfluenced by too much wood, try a Médoc that is mainly matured in old wood such as La Tour de By, Latour St Bonnet, or La Cardonne (no wood); alternatively Domaine de Gaillat or Château Chicane from the Graves, or a generic "Médoc". For a finer, and perhaps more typical version with the cedar/vanilla character, almost any Classed Growth or good Cru Bourgeois will do: Les Forts de Latour is an excellent alternative to the

Grand Vin of Château Latour; Clos du Marquis or Potensac (from the Lascases stable), Chasse Spleen, Lannessan, Sénéjac; or La Louvière or Bouscaut from the Graves. For a 100 per cent new oak wine that won't cost a fortune try Château Haut Marbuzet. Some people love it for its early, overt blackcurrant and vanilla flavour; others, myself included, find it vulgar when young, and too drily astringent as it ages. It is certainly "oaky", and worth trying. As these left bank wines mature, the bouquet softens and heads for a "cassis" or "cooked mulberry" character; the oak is less obviously vanillary and more "cedary", and the fine earthiness is often more pronounced as well. A "vertical" tasting of young and old vintages of any one property is the best way to demonstrate this.

Trying to distinguish between the communes of St-Estephe, Pauillac, St Julien, Margaux and Graves is easier the better the vintage, the younger the wine and the finer its quality. Differences in grape mix, vintage and winemaking style mean that the borders can never be absolutely clear cut, and most blind tasters are quite happy just to have placed the wine on the correct side of the river.

(**Above**) *One of wine's unsolved mysteries: the ultimate source of quality, or what accounts for the difference between a First Growth and a Second Growth château? Only a "jalle", a trickling stream, separates the vineyard of Château Latour, on the left, from that of Leoville Las Cases on the right. Yet Latour's best will always have the quality edge over the best of Las Cases.*

(**Above**) *The eighteenth century elegance of Château Beychevelle in St Julien. From the main road you only see the back of the property; this is the front, facing the river.*

Nevertheless, there are broad differences which it is interesting to try and perceive. At the "top" of the Médoc map is St-Estephe, whose cool clayey soil tends to produce wines that are fruity but sturdy, often with both high acidity and lots of tannin, and slightly coarse earthy character. Pauillac wines have the highest proportion of Cabernet Sauvignon, and are intense, assertive, concentratedly blackcurrant in flavour, with a noticeable spicy element. St Julien is usually the most elegantly proportioned; less tannic than the two previous communes, particularly cedary in flavour – most people's idea of classic claret. Both Margaux and Graves have a higher proportion of Merlot and generally make wines of more moderate concentration – they are easy to confuse (congratulate yourself if you have narrowed the options this far!). Margaux often has a particularly perfumed bouquet, a softer, silkier feel; Graves tend to be more open knit in texture and to have a pronounced but fine, dry earthiness, part flavour, part texture. Good hunting!

Cabernet Sauvignon is little represented elsewhere in France. From the Loire a small proportion bolsters the raspberry freshness of Cabernet Franc in Bourgueil, and it is increasingly used as an "improving" grape in

the south of France (L'Hérault and L'Aude). Château Vignelaure from Aix-en-Provence contains over 50 per cent in its grape mix and in addition to the cassis and mulberry bouquet, it shows how Cabernet fills out and enriches the soft, but diffuse blend of Grenache, Cinsaut and Carignan. An interesting oddball from L'Hérault is the slow to mellow Mas de Daumas Gassac: 80 per cent Cabernet Sauvignon plus Merlot and a host of other grapes in tiny amounts. It has been described, over enthusiastically, as the "Lafite" of the Midi. Try it for jammy blackcurrant Cabernet and marked oak tannin rather than in the hopes of a Lafite lookalike.

Outside France Cabernet Sauvignon wines can be divided into two very broad groups: those that are moderately concentrated, fruity in flavour, relatively supple for the variety, with little wood influence and little tannin. These are principally to be found in northeast Italy, eastern Europe, South America and South Africa. The second group consists of more concentrated and more tannic wines that are clearly marked by oak-ageing; sweet and vanillary in the case of American oak, subtler in their wood spice where French oak is used. Wines in this group come from

Spain, Portugal, central Italy, California, Australia and, to a lesser extent, New Zealand.

Bulgaria's Cabernet Sauvignons are amongst the cheapest one can buy, but they will show you quintessential blackcurrant-jam Cabernet at its plump, soft and gulpable simplest; and for just a few pence more they will provide another bottle to show how small-oak ageing affects this fruity simplicity, giving it a drier edge, a little more spice, astringency and interest. The best come from Svishtov and Suhindol in the north, Sakar in the south, and so far their oak doesn't overwhelm the Cabernet fruit with vanilla sweetness.

Northeast Italy's Cabernet Sauvignons include supple, plummy, straightforward wines for early drinking from Friuli-Venezia-Giulia; and drier, slightly spicier styles from the Veneto, an area which also boasts an extraordinary Bordeaux lookalike: Venegazzu. This is a Médoc blend of grapes, producing a wine which, at about four years old, smells and tastes like a mellow, mature Bordeaux: soft and warm, with a sweet, rich mulberry flavour. Only its fluid feel and a touch of carbon dioxide tells you it can't be what you first think it is! Further north, in the Alto Adige (South Tyrol) the Cabernets, even when identified as "Sauvignon" often have a distinctly briary-earthy Cabernet "Franc" smell to them, with only a slightly "green", herby character recalling Sauvignon. These are fresh, lively wines; dry and flavoury with much less of Bulgaria's blackcurrant sweetness. None of these suggest much wood contact, and certainly no new oak.

The Cabernet Sauvignons from South Africa and South America, though they spend more time in wood remain very low in tannin (the wood is old) and free from new oak character. Supple, easy drinking is what sells well locally, hence the style. The best South American examples come from Chile, and the pick of these from the Maipo Valley: Cousino Macul's Antiguas Reservas especially, and the Concha y Toro wines. Cabernet here smells blackcurrant-sweet with a suggestion of oil and minerals; in texture the wines are remarkably soft, almost slick, and their plentiful ripe, easy fruit often finishes with an echo of the minerally-volcanic spice aroma smelled on the nose. South African Cabernet Sauvignons have a similarly mellow, fluid character and smooth-sweet flavour, although usually with a little more acidity and a gently peppery, earthy aftertaste. The wines are full, but rarely concentrated, not even the fine "Bordeaux" style Meerlust Rubicon. New-oak ageing is just beginning to creep in.

The second, and much larger, group of non-French Cabernet Sauvignons are all "new-oaked" in small barrels to a greater or lesser extent. For Spain read American oak, very largely; and for central Italy, French and/or Slavonian oak. A clear and inexpensive introduction to the influence of American oak (as a foil to those two Bulgarians perhaps) would be Raimat's Cabernet Sauvignon from Lerida in Spain, or Fonseca's Quinta do Bacalhoa from southern Portugal. In comparison to the unwooded Bulgarian look for the sweet vanilla topping to the blackcurrant nose, the additional sweetness of taste and a spicy dryness of texture from the oak tannin. The appeal is immediate and obvious. In a more refined vein are two wines from Penedès; Torres' Gran Coronas Black Label, (between 90 and 100 per cent Cabernet Sauvignon) and Jean León's Cabernet Sauvignon. The Torres wine is a finely textured, elegant medium-weight, more subtly vanillary than the Raimat, but still "American-oaked" in style; the León however is a harder, more concentrated and more tannic wine, and its oak is French, little of it new. The contrast is clear and striking: no vanilla, less sweetness and a taste of older wood.

You could make this a (much) more costly, but deliciously five star comparison by adding two top

(**Below**) *The sterile façade of modern winemaking with integral, double skinned stainless steel jackets for temperature control, and sloping bottoms to facilitate removal of the skins. This vat room could be anywhere in the world with serious winemaking ambitions and money to invest. It is in fact at the no-expense-spared Jordan Vineyard in Alexander Valley, California.*

(**Right**) *Vineyards at the Mondavi winery in California's Napa Valley, viewed through one of the arches of the Franciscan mission style building. Mondavi's are benchmark Californian wines; a consequence of considerable investment allied to continual, passionate experiment and a very clear concept of balance in a style that avoids any excess.*

(**Below right**) *French expertise abroad, at Forman Winery in California. When building his winery in the early 'eighties Ric Forman imported French coopers to make his vats and barrels, using exclusively French oak. Mondavi also uses only French oak, but most California wineries use a blend of French and American wood.*

quality central Italians, Sassicaia (100 per cent Cabernet Sauvignon) and Antinori's Solaia (75 per cent Cabernet Sauvignon, 25 per cent Cabernet Franc). The Sassicaia is an intense, concentrated blackcurrant essence; the Solaia a more refined and complex style. These are both aged in new French oak, giving the wines a drier, spicier, more fine grained tannic quality. With a bit of age the Solaia in particular has the "cedary" quality produced by new French oak.

Trying to generalize about Californian and Australian Cabernets is even more hazardous than doing the same for Bordeaux. For each group the areas covered are vast, the variations in climate and soil considerable, consistent patterns and styles often barely established. In the late seventies there was a period where, possibly with Mouton Rothschild and La Mission Haut Brion as models, the almost universal Californian goal seemed to be to out-Cabernet Bordeaux; if some was good, more was better, for fruit extract and tannin in particular, and many wines were inky, alcoholic, thick and astringent. Wines which will need decades to mellow, but which are more likely to remain coarse and blunt for ever. Today's approach is much more moderate. Overall the wines remain more forceful than their European and even Australian counterparts. Colour is typically very deep, and the Cabernet Sauvignon smells blackcurrant "jammy" in basic wines. Better wines often

have a hint of mint on the blackcurrant and frequently suggest greenery as well, whether this be "bellpepper" (green pepper) freshness or a more bruised, "weedy", vegetal character which is quite unlike any Cabernets from Europe or Australia. In contrast to the latter their flavour tends to be fatter, stronger, less sweet and more earthy and herbaceous (although often richly blackcurranty). Their texture is generally more tannic with the acidity less apparent, and they finish drier. Oak is often not that prominent, and the wines are generally much less approachable young than the Australians are. They need time, but yes,

(**Left**) *The famous "Terra Rossa" strip of soil at Coonawarra in South Australia, a rectangle $9\frac{1}{2}$ miles long by a mile wide, producing two-thirds of Australia's Cabernet Sauvignon in a particularly elegant style.*

they do age well. If you have any doubts, try a good quality Californian from the 1974 or 1975 vintage. At twelve years old, 1974 Caymus and Beaulieu Vineyards George de Latour Private Reserve, showed just how polished and harmonious they can be given time. Firestone's 1975 at the same age had the bouquet, flavour and mellowness of texture that would make one coo with satisfaction if it were a twelve-year-old Cru Bourgeois claret!

A cross section of wines to show California Cabernet Sauvignon styles could include Mondavi's or Stag's Leap's middleweight elegance; the rich, oaky, showy Trefethen, forcefully minty and complex Martha's Vineyard, the concentrated and tannic Phelps — all Napa wines; Iron Horse, Kenwood or Jordan from Sonoma: stylish, lighter Californians; and the reliable, minerally blackcurrant Firestone from Santa Barbara. A recent trend is away from pure Cabernet Sauvignon to a blend with Merlot and/or Cabernet Franc, aged in new French oak. The aim is to produce a style that is both more complex and more elegant. Opus 1 and Insignia are obvious examples, Carmenet from Sonoma another that is extremely good and less expensive.

Australian Cabernets offer everything from a juicy gulp to long, complex velvety refinement. Their enormous advantage over the majority of Californian and European Cabernet Sauvignons is that many of the best are approachable and delicious very early on, and yet they lack for nothing in structure or finesse. Their red often has a blackish hue, and for California's minty nose read eucalyptus here, over a gentler blackcurrant often marked by a particularly sweet oak vanilla, also clear on the palate. They are less concentrated, extracty and tannic than most Californians, more flowing and easier to drink. Their acidity is fresher, indeed it sometimes has a hint of the citrus character more often associated with the white wines. Australian Cabernets fall a little more easily into area styles than the Californians. The New South Wales Hunter Valley wines are some of Australia's most solid and tannic Cabernets. Their "bouquet" includes smells that are earthy, oily, volcanic, baked (kinder descriptions of what is locally known as "sweaty saddle"). They can be full and rich, but also rather blunt; finesse is not their strong point (Tyrrells, Rothbury Estate, Rosemount). Notable exceptions to the latter generalization are Allandale's beautiful blackcurranty Cabernet and Robson Vineyard's elegant, savoury wine. Unlike the Chardonnay, I am at a loss to understand the admiration for Lakes Folly Cabernet in the 1983 and 1985 vintages at least (I do not know any earlier ones); I have found them dilute, stewed and dull, entirely lacking the appeal and complexity that its reputation implies. Will someone explain the quality to me please? Victoria produces some ripe and powerful Cabernets with a distinct mint-eucalyptus nose such as Balgownie, and Brown Brothers Koombahla; but in a quite different, leaner, drier style, from cooler areas, are such wines as Tisdall's Mount Helen; and, from the Yarra Valley, Yarra Burn and Mount Mary Vineyard "Cabernets", a beautifully balanced, subtle and aromatic wine in a deliberately "European" style.

Nearly two thirds of Australia's Cabernet Sauvignon comes from Coonawarra, South Australia; an area with a mild climate and a famous strip of "terra rossa" soil, red loam over limestone. Cabernets here are more medium-bodied wines, notable for their balanced proportions and elegant, even tasting qualities. They are moderate in colour, with less mint on the nose, but more of a classic Cabernet black-currant, earth and cedar. Their tannin is generally fine in texture and their flavour long and lingering. Along with the Margaret River wines, these constitute Australia's classiest Cabernet Sauvignons. Numerous lovely wines, but to select a few plums: Mildara: dry, firm and even; Leconfield, long, elegant and cedary; Hungerford Hill, rich and oaky; Petaluma, under-stated, refined; Wynn's standard Cabernet is very good, their John Riddoch an elegant, concentrated Cabernet to match the finest from Europe or America.

Western Australia's Margaret River, another cool area, is producing some stunning wines, in all too limited quantity. Leeuwin and Vasse Felix both produce fine textured, tight knit Cabernets; the former softer and sweeter; the latter aromatic, austere and "dry" in flavour for Australia. Moss Wood's is one of the most seductive wines you could wish for: velvety textured, cedary blackcurrant, dense, complex and polished. Australian Cabernet is quite often blended with Shiraz in order to "fill out the middle palate". I think the best Cabernets manage perfectly well by themselves. The Cabernet-Shiraz wines are good wines in their own right, tending to be broader and spicier, not "better" Cabernets. Good ones to try are those from Berri Estates, Penfolds (St Henri), Mildara, Wolf Blass and Idyll Vineyard.

New Zealand's Cabernet Sauvignons are a mixed bunch at present. Cabernet Sauvignon often seems to masquerade as Cabernet Franc, smelling grassy, briary and fresh. On the palate they are generally lively, sometimes tart and without much depth — as yet. Where there is a lot of extract the wine tends to be too tough. Cooks is one of the most attractive (black-currant and American oak), Matua Valley and Montana are in a lighter vein, though the 1986 Matua shows the exciting potential of New Zealand Cabernets.

PINOT NOIR

Pinot Noir is the sole grape from which red Burgundy is made. Occasionally it produces a wine that for sheer, overwhelming sensual pleasure and elaborate flavours leaves all other wines standing. It is only the ravishing impact of one of these, and knowing that it does exist at all that keeps hope alive in the Pandora's box of evil bottles that regularly disappoint in the name of Pinot Noir or one of Burgundy's maze of appellations.

One explanation for its inconsistency is that, amongst a whole host of different clones, its "quality" clone in Burgundy, the Pinot Fin or Pinot Tordu ("fine" or "twisted"), is prone to disease and low in yield, whereas the alternative, Pinot Droit, is both more practical to grow and more productive, but its wine is a pallid version of the "Fin". In "grape farm" terminology the crude distinction might be "Pinot Fin good, Pinot Droit bad", and sadly there are a large number of mature Pinot Droit vines in Burgundy. But even with the best clones, finely balanced Pinot wine is difficult to achieve; and no amount of explanation can make up for the frustration of expensive bottles that fail to live up to expectations!

In addition to the Burgundian clone merry-go-round there are the hazards of grower/shipper roulette. What matters a great deal more than the name of the wine in the vineyard hierarchy is the name of those who tended the vines and/or made the wine. *Whose* Burgundy rather than *which* Burgundy. With all these variables and the difficulty of even making an attractive let alone a "typical" Pinot outside France, no wonder it is hard to come up with a model example.

In Burgundy, Pinot generally produces a wine that is moderate in colour, and has more acid than tannin (1983 is an exception where the wines tend to be rich in both colour and tannin). The smell of Pinot is notoriously difficult to describe, if less so to recognize. When young its fruit character is of cherries and raspberries, "sweet" and "smooth" in comparison to Cabernet Sauvignon or Syrah, but there is often a smokey side to it as well. At a comparable quality level it matures more rapidly than Claret or northern Rhône, most are quite ready at ten years, many much earlier. Its bouquet then takes on an added and distinctly vegetal, sometimes "gamey" character; a mixture of sweet and rotten, fragrant and fumy. Its mature flavour is "sweet", but not sugary, its consistency silky smooth yet fresh with a very fine grain tannin and a delicate spiciness which develops at length and lingers long on the aftertaste. When the balance is right its appeal lies in a unique combination of delicacy and power, where even intensely rich and concentrated wines do not feel "thick".

Burgundy's Côte d'Or, the golden slope, is the uncontested source of the world's finest Pinot Noirs. Wines from its northern half, the Côte de Nuits, are usually characterized as being more weighty wines: firmer, spicier, more pungent and minerally than those of the Côte de Beaune. The latter's are reckoned to be lighter, more flowery and supple, quicker to develop and fade. Useful as these generalizations are in broad terms, there will be many exceptions, and as often as not these will be due to the hand of the winemaker. You can get a good idea of commune differences by comparing the range of wines from a reliable merchant such as Drouhin, Jadot or Bouchard Père et Fils; but for something more exciting and individual, "growers" are a better bet: Dujac, Lignier, Bertagna, Jayer, Simon Bize, Rion, Lafon and Domaine de La Pousse d'Or are some to look out for.

Just south of the Côte d'Or, the Chalonnais or Région de Mercurey wines can provide more affordable if less exalted examples of Pinot to demonstrate its basic bouquet, flavour and balance. Mercurey is the most reliable (as well as the largest production), Givry perhaps a bit more distinguished; Rully is better

known for its whites. Producers to look out for are Delorme (Domaine de La Renarde), Juillot and Chandesais.

Alsatian Pinot Noir is pale and fresh, full bodied and silky textured without being deep in flavour and it almost always has a particularly clear and perfumed Pinot nose – a good way to get to know the (unoaked) basic smell! Sancerre can produce some attractive, chalky Pinot Noirs in sunny seasons (try Vacheron's); those from the Jura tend to be thin and somewhat astringent. Pinot Noir accounts for a third of the grapes grown in Champagne where it makes a little sharply refreshing Bouzy Rouge when it is not

(**Below**) *Pinot Noir. A tightly clustered bunch like this nicely demonstrates the pine cone shape from which the grape derives its name. And their perfect condition and ripeness is that of 1985, one of those all too rare vintages that produced fabulous red Burgundy.*

used for Champagne itself.

Outside France, but still in Europe, there is little Pinot that will excite the taste buds. The best Italian versions are from the South Tyrol, where they can be well coloured, sweet, fragrant and lightly tannic if without much depth or interest on the palate. Germany's Spätburgunder, mainly from Assmanshausen in the Rheingau and from Baden and the Rheinpfalz, is rarely absolutely dry, but sweetish; best drunk cool and soon. Dôle from Switzerland is a blend of Pinot and Gamay, but they make pure Pinot as well, at its best from the Valais; here it can be sweet fruited, light and faintly minerally, almost devoid of tannin, occasionally quite fine. More often it is whisker clean, urbane but empty.

So far Pinot has defeated the efforts of the majority of winemakers outside France to come up with the same sort of magic that Burgundy occasionally produces. Whereas Cabernet Sauvignon responds well to a warm climate and can make a virtue of concentration, the essential appeal of Pinot, its delicacy and fine texture, is lost as soon as growing conditions are too warm and the wine too robust and plummy.

If Californian efforts have only met with moderate success north of San Francisco (in the Alexander and Carneros Valleys especially; try Joseph Swan and Iron Horse from the former, Acacia from the latter), cooler

(**Right**) *Looking south to the village of Vosne Romanée, over some of the most valuable vineyards on earth, those of the Domaine de la Romanée Conti. This view shows perfectly the lie of Burgundy's Côte d'Or (the golden slope). The basic "commune" appellation vineyards are to the right of the picture, high up the slope, and again low down on the flat beyond the village. In between, in the hillside's "navel", are the quality vineyards; in this case the top quality Grand Cru vineyard of Richebourg beyond the long wall, and second rank, Premier Cru vineyards, on either side of the road in the foreground.*

pale (like a 1982 Burgundy for example) and their bouquets a light, smoky Pinot style often with a distinct earthy/minerally character. They are quite full in alcohol with a marked fresh acidity and very light dry tannin. Their flavours are dry, only moderate in depth but with a subtle, noticeable minerally spice on the palate and on long aromatic finishes; a consistent reflection of the bouquet. Perhaps this minerally character has something to do with the proximity of the volcanic Cascade mountain range?

These are well defined wines, subtly oaked, with pure, clear cut flavours but lacking a little ripeness and flesh at the moment. This is especially so in cooler years (1984) where their delicacy verges on the watery. Rather cold, if quite refined personalities! Tualatin is one of the most complete; Eyrie, Alpine, Elk Cove and Knudsen Erath all very good examples too. Elk Cove is the only wine on which I have ever smelt a distinct whiff of Marijuana . . ! Will this be a hallmark of some Oregon wines in the way that eucalyptus from the gum trees marks out Martha's Vineyard in the Napa Valley for example?

South Africa produces little pure Pinot Noir, and where they do it is suave and supple but a bit bland. Much more common is their Pinotage wine (a crossing of Pinot Noir and Cinsaut) which makes a soft, full, sweetish wine with a gently spicy character.

Australia's production of Pinot Noir wine is also limited, but there are some really exciting wines which promise well for the future of this grape down under. Tyrrell produce an oaky and rather severe wine in the Hunter Valley, very variable according to the vintage; but Robson's Hunter Valley Pinot (alas only 400 cases as yet) is something special: mint and eucalyptus on the nose, slightly tarry flavoured, tight knit, smoky wine. Tisdall's Mount Helen's is another highly rated wine which I (again) cannot come to terms with. I find it a weird concoction of high acid and aggressive oak with an almost sickly intensity of sweet vanilla. Try it, I think it's a "you either love it or hate it" wine. One of Victoria's most exciting Pinots is Mount Mary's from the Yarra Valley. This is an opulent and racy wine, fine textured, intricately flavoured and without a trace of vulgarity. Also very good are the Moss Wood and Leeuwin Pinot Noirs from Western Australia; the former firm and sweetly oaky, the latter an elegant, ripe and spicy medium weight wine. The cooler New Zealand climate suggests that it should produce good Pinots eventually, at present many are tough and lean, Nobilo's is the most successful, Montana's also good.

areas south of the bay are much more promising. Here, on the eastern side of the Salinas Valley Chalone makes a dark, rich and mouthfilling Pinot Noir which, for all its weight, has considerable finesse. Calera's Jensen Vineyard Pinot Noir from a little further north is a big, firm, flavoury wine; minerally, aromatic and with excellent length, and very distinctly Pinot. Heading south again, the Edna Valley wine is not concentrated but has all the hallmarks of good Pinot: smoky bouquet, fine sweet fruit in a silken texture and a soft, spicy finish. From the Napa Valley Mondavi's Pinot is always reliable: firm, oaky, herbaceous; Trefethen's is a bigger wine, always very oaky.

Oregon has been enthusiastically described as Pinot Noir's second home. I do not find the wines as Burgundian as some do, but they are certainly distinctive and individual. As yet my enthusiasm for them, and to be fair my experience of them, is limited. However I have found a very consistent style. The majority of wines come from the Willamette Valley, south of Portland, where the growing season is long and the climate a cool continental one. Their colour is

SYRAH

Syrah is rightly regarded as one of the noblest red grape varieties, and yet its quality wine production is limited to the northern Rhône in France, to parts of Australia and to just a few wines from California. What makes this even more puzzling is that not only is it a fairly easy grape to grow, but in the mid nineteenth century its northern Rhône wines were as highly sought after as First Growth Claret and Grand Cru Burgundy. Today the quality of its finest wines, from France or Australia, remains equal to anything that Cabernet Sauvignon or Pinot Noir can produce. Possibly the extremely limited quantities of its top wines are the very reason for its not being more widely planted; it simply isn't widely enough known to be in great demand. However, the northern Rhône wines are once again becoming more fashionable and the best Australian Shiraz wines are deservedly recognized as excellent. It would be nice then to think that in future Syrah could divert some of the attention given to the relentlessly global invasion of Cabernet Sauvignon.

In the northern Rhône, Syrah's small thick skinned grape produces wines with plenty of alcohol, tannin and acidity; it is often this combination of firm tannin and high acidity that marks them out when tasted blind. (Nebbiolo has a similar constitution but is usually more astringent and tarry in flavour.) The finest wines are those from the Hermitage hill and the precipitous slopes of Côte Rôtie 30 miles further north. Although the Hermitage appellation laws allow

for up to 15 per cent of white grapes, in practice red Hermitage is made from pure Syrah. The wines are dark purple and the nose of young Syrah here is peppery, minerally, often with a suggestion of cassis in a hot year. Although firm and tannic, Hermitage is surprisingly elegant with a long even, highly wrought development of spicy, minerally, smoky blackcurrant flavours. It is a denser, sterner seeming wine than Côte Rôtie, more mouthcoating and with more obvious fruit extract. Mature wines, with a minimum of ten to 15 years in bottle, have a wonderfully penetrating soft and sweet blackcurrant bouquet and a velvety sweetness of flavour that is hard to imagine in their youth. Jaboulet's "La Chapelle' and Chave's wine are the two touchstone Hermitages.

Côte Rôtie is allowed up to 20 per cent of the white Viognier grape to be blended with Syrah, but as the whole appellation only contains 5–6 per cent Viognier the proportion is always very much less, if there at all. With or without Viognier (and more so with), Côte Rôtie is often somewhat paler than Hermitage, and both more fragrant and more smoky, roasted and singed to smell. To taste, mature Côte Rôtie is fiery but not fierce, more delicate than Hermitage and with a particularly elaborate, spicy development that easily matches the complexity of the finest Claret or Burgundy. Guigal is one of the best producers, but Pierre and Gilles Barge, Rostaing, Champet, Jasmin and Jaboulet's Côte Rôtie "Les Jumelles" are all worth looking out for.

Crozes-Hermitage and St Joseph are slighter expressions of northern Rhône Syrah but in a similar

(**Below**) *Syrah grapes on the Hermitage Hill; small and thick skinned, and therefore with a high ratio of colour and tannin to juice, they make a concentrated, tannic wine. The grapes literally bake in the sun. I photographed these at 6pm on a September evening, at well over 30°C. Still basking in the sunlight, they were remarkably hot to the touch. No wonder "roasted" so often springs to mind when tasting these wines.*

(**Below right**) *Looking south west from the Hermitage hill, over the village of Tain l'Hermitage and the Rhône river, towards the flatter landscape of the southern Rhône.*

COTE ROTIE CHAPOUTIER

CÔTE-RÔTIE E. GUIGAL

vein, with noticeably earthy, peppery flavours. When young, and particularly from young vines, the grape in these wines may smell somewhat "green", often reminiscent of green, unroasted coffee beans. Cornas, the remaining pure Syrah wine, can have the concentration of fine Hermitage without its elegance and complexity. Although more straightforward, it usually has a wonderful concentration of ripe, fiery blackcurrant fruit; Clape, Barjac, Michel and Jaboulet are the ones to try.

In California Joseph Phelps used to be about the only name one could mention as making a respectable Syrah wine; even these are very variable. His 1977 was a strong, rich, roasted and spicy wine with a distinct varietal character, but both earlier and later wines have been much lighter and less interesting. Although I have never tasted it myself, Bonny Doon is highly rated by Robert Parker.

Australia is the other main source of Syrah wines, here called Shiraz, but even as an expert you would often be hard put to see the Syrah connection! For there are vast quantities of anonymous, watery quaffing Shiraz from high yields and precious little of anything that resembles the concentrated fruit and the peppery, roasted flavours that are so individual in the northern Rhône wines. But a small proportion of distinctive wines show just how good Shiraz can be in Australia. These are in a style quite different from the French Syrah, tending more towards Châteauneuf sweetness and softness than northern Rhône density, elegance and firmness. And there are varying styles of Shiraz within Australia itself.

Hunter Valley Shiraz tend to be particularly warm and richly sweet in flavour, smooth and soft in texture, often with a mouthcoating, almost sticky feel on the finish; good examples are produced by Rose-

(**Above**) *Space is at a premium on the pincushion slopes above Ampuis in the Côte Rôtie. The terraces have single rows of vines and the Côte Rôtie "wigwam" or inverted "V" staking on which the vines are trained.*

(**Right**) *Penfolds original estate at Magill – the source of a great Syrah wine – on the outskirts of Adelaide, now swamped by urban sprawl. Until 1970 Penfolds top wine, Grange Hermitage, was made entirely from Shiraz vines here. Their new wine, Magill Estate, is still made from the small area of Shiraz vineyard remaining (foreground).*

(**Above**) *Guigal's La Landonne vineyard in Côte Rôtie. This plot, bought from 17 growers over a period of 10 years, is an unbroken, unterraced single hectare face which plunges down to road and river at an angle of 65°. It makes a dramatic, oaky, elaborate and highly sought after Syrah wine.*

mount, Rothbury and MacWilliams; a more forceful and spicy wine by Robson. Western Australia looks as though it may yield some exciting Shiraz although there are too few, with too short a history, to say with any certainty. Peel Estate's Shiraz from south of Perth is very dry, concentrated and fairly tannic; Plantagenet is full, peppery and fairly oaky too. Cape Mentelle's wine has the minerally spice and firm acidity of Rhône Syrah, if not yet its complexity.

The most successful Shiraz come from South Australia and Victoria. Penfolds Grange Hermitage (Hermitage is the "old" name for Shiraz here) is Australia's most illustrious red; a mouthfillingly rich blend of ripe, chocolatey fruit and oak with an almost viscous consistency. Penfold's Kalimna Bin 28 is plump, oaky, easy, a mellow medium weight, but for a really exciting wine try their new baby, the Magill Estate Shiraz. Until the early 1970's this provided between a half and two thirds of the grapes for the Grange Hermitage, but a large part of the vineyard is now an Adelaide suburb. 1983 saw the first "Magill" wine, from old vines and aged in 100 per cent new Limousin oak. Its virtues are those of elegance and complexity rather than strength or particular forcefulness; it is a beautifully balanced wine with exceptional development and length. Curiously, the 1984 is a leaner and less impressive wine. Another estate to watch in South Australia is that of Adams and Wray whose first Shiraz (1986) is a firm, deep, savoury wine, noticeably influenced by oak; very good quality if not in the league of Grange or Magill.

I think the most distinctive Australian Shiraz comes from Victoria, the central highland district in particular. Taltarni's is strong, blackcurranty and full of spice; Cathcart Ridge is also a potent mint and eucalyptus wine; liquoricey, tannic, characterful; most distinctive of all though is Mount Langhi Ghiran; dry, earthy, peppery, volcanic; not at all the sweet, smooth Shiraz style and all the more interesting for not being so; and Yarra Yering No 2 Dry Red is another peppery-dry Shiraz in this vein.

MERLOT

There is much more Merlot grown in Bordeaux than Cabernet Sauvignon. But whereas Cabernet's image is that of tannin bound austerity, very much the backbone of Médoc aristocracy, Merlot's role is seen as tempering Cabernet's firmness and putting flesh on its backbone. And it is Merlot that accounts for Pomerol's "fleshy" image and St Emilion's reputation as the beguiling "Burgundy" of Bordeaux. These impressions of softness and sensual appeal mean that Merlot is rarely viewed with the same reverence as Cabernet Sauvignon, at least not by those for whom the puritanical appeal of Cabernet is more proper. It is as though Merlot's sensuality is suspect, as though she conferred her favours too easily to be a real aristocrat. Petrus' almost 100 per cent Merlot personality is another matter. The greatest courtesans are always highly valued, and if not considered quite true aristocrats, they are at least above morality.

Merlot is a larger, thinner skinned grape than Cabernet Sauvignon and the wine it produces is usually plentiful in alcohol but only moderately tannic. Its wines have the advantage of being rich yet relatively supple and therefore drinkable from early on. Like Grenache in the southern Rhône, Merlot's deep, bright purple in youth soon "browns" at the edges, often a clue to its identity. In its most com-

monly encountered form as a half to two thirds of the St Emilion blend (the balance being largely Cabernet Franc) Merlot smells sweet and smoothly fruity, without the earthy edge of Cabernet. With a bit of age this can become farmyardy, sometimes suggesting the mealy character of coarse ground grain or the more vegetal odour of mown hay or mushrooms. I also find Jancis Robinson's "fruitcake" description is a very useful one. In a concentrated Pomerol, where it will usually account for at least two thirds of the grapes (the balance again being principally Cabernet Franc) it can seem almost buttery or creamy on the nose.

On the palate Merlot seems softer, warmer (it is usually higher in alcohol) and sweeter than Cabernet with a looser, more open and smoother texture. Its

(**Above**) Merlot, the sybarite's grape; all soft gratification . . . that, at least, is the image.
(**Left**) This unhurried, bucolic image from the past is current reality at Château Ausone, St Emilion. The grey mare, Hermine, has for years been drawing the plough on those parts of the vineyard where it is impractical to work mechanically.

(**Far right**) *A frosty January morning in Pomerol. The dried vine shoots will be used as fuel for cooking; lit and reduced to a glowing char over which meat and fish are singed* (**above**).
(**Right**) *Château Petrus's eponymous saint praising the lord . . . and banking the cheques?*

most opulent wines, Pomerols in particular, have an almost chocolatey flavour with an exotic spiciness. One of the problems in trying to tie down Merlot's personality is that its yield varies considerably and it can be, and indeed often is, very large. The wines are then dilute and vapid. St Emilions range from plenty of this kind to the concentration of Château Canon or L'Arrosée. And though Merlot is generally thought of as not very tannic and especially fleshy in Pomerol, much depends on the soil in which it is grown. Château de Sales or Clos René from lighter, sandier soils do make generous, supple, plummy Pomerols with very little tannin; wines like Nenin, Beauregard or Le Gay on the other hand can often have a fair whack of tannin. La Graves Trigant de Boisset and La Conseillante are wines that fit the silky textured image if not the one of concentration; the velvety, mouthcoating richness of Petrus, Trotanoy or Evangile is by no means the norm, but due in a large part to their heavier, more clayey soil, which is too cold for Cabernet to ripen in, but in which Merlot thrives.

Merlot will usually be the main grape in a host of smaller appellations on the "Right Bank" in the Bordeaux region: the so called "satellite" St Emilions; the Pomerol fringes, Néac and Lalande de Pomerol; the Fronsac wines and those from Bourg, Blaye and the Premier Côtes de Bordeaux.

Bulgaria produces good basic buttery Merlot, Yugoslavia some rather jammy examples. Northeast Italy's versions vary from a high yield, watery neutrality to light, fresh, fruity wines from the Veneto and Friuli. As yet there is little in Portugal and Spain, although Spain's Raimat makes an award winning oaky Merlot just as good as its Lerida Cabernet.

Outside Europe Merlot is nothing like as popular as Cabernet Sauvignon. It is beginning to make an appearance as a single varietal in the cooler areas of Australia and it is also occasionally blended with Cabernet there. In the United States its best wines come from Washington (Château Ste Michelle) and California. Good Californian Merlots are dark, rich and strong (Cuvaison, Duckhorn, Clos du Bois for example) but they can also be coarsely tannic in comparison with their French counterparts.

CABERNET FRANC

Cabernet Franc is seen at its most distinctive in France in the Loire vineyards of Anjou, Saumur and Touraine; at its most lush and aristocratic in its two thirds contribution to St Emilion's Château Cheval Blanc; and its role in the quality of Bordeaux's blend is certainly underestimated. There is very little planted in Australia or South Africa and it is rarely seen as a single varietal in the Americas, although it is growing in importance in California with the move away from 100 per cent Cabernet Sauvignon wines and towards blends that are lighter, more subtle and more elegant. The only other area where it is vinified as a varietal wine is in northeast Italy. In the cool regions of New Zealand and Tasmania it is often difficult to tell whether a wine is made from Cabernet Sauvignon or Cabernet Franc. Most of it *tastes* like the latter.

When not in New Zealand or Tasmania, how does it differ from Cabernet Sauvignon? It is a larger, thinner skinned grape and its wine is less tannic, less concentrated and usually paler in colour; what it has more of is acidity. In a Chinon or a Saumur Champigny from the Loire its smell resembles raspberries or violets rather than blackcurrant and its fruit character is fresher and more piquant. What distinguishes it even more clearly here though is its aromatic character which is herbaceous and grassy, and for me it often has a marked but fine earthy-chalky character. This is sometimes so aggressive as to smell almost dusty. To taste it is light, fresh, sweet and flavoury.

In Bordeaux it accounts for up to 25 per cent of a Médoc blend (more typically 10–20 per cent), 25–50 per cent of a St Emilion make-up; and lighter wines from the Premier Côtes; Bourg, Blaye and Bergerac often have the more fluid, flavoury feel of a high proportion of Cabernet Franc. Particularly interesting is to see just how significant it is in the Left Bank wines. Several chateaux bottle a small amount of the individual grape varieties separately; De Pez did in 1970, Leoville Lascases did between 1979 and 1983. Tasted separately Cabernet Franc certainly lacks concentration, weight and tannin next to Cabernet Sauvignon, but it more than makes up for this with a remarkable fragrance on the nose, finesse on the palate and length on the finish. In a blend it not only softens the Sauvignon's tannic austerity but it adds complexity, definition and development to the middle palate; aromatic interest to the aftertaste. A comparison like this shows just why it is gaining popularity for blending with Californian Cabernet Sauvignons.

CHÂTEAU CHEVAL BLANC
·1975·
St Emilion
1ᵉʳ Grand Cru Classé
HÉRITIERS FOURCAUD-LAUSSAC
PROPRIÉTAIRES
Mis en bouteille au Château   (FRANCE)
APPELLATION SAINT-ÉMILION 1ᵉʳ GRAND CRU CLASSÉ CONTROLÉE 73cl
PRODUCE OF FRANCE

(**Left**) *Cheval Blanc has a surprising 66% Cabernet Franc in its blend, and the wine shows just how refined the grape can be.* (**Below**) *Ripe Cabernet Franc with the vine already in autumn dress.*

(**Right**) *Barbaresco in Piedmont, northern Italy. One of the countless hilltop villages of the region, whose all round view once made ideal defensive positions and now makes them wonderful "bel-vederes". No room for urban sprawl here, and their cramped, cobbled streets, weathered Sienna tiles and aura of stillness seem barely to have changed since the middle ages.*

NEBBIOLO

"Nebbioso", meaning foggy, describes the state of Piedmont's slopes in late October. It is the time when the Nebbiolo grape is ready to be picked, hence its name. A local name for a very local grape, because Nebbiolo is, for all practical purposes, exclusive to this north western corner of Italy where it makes Barolo and Barbaresco and a host of other lesser wines with devilish names like Sassello, Grumello, Inferno and so on.

Their deep, concentrated, almost bitter-burnt flavour is starkly framed by a fierce, dry, mouthcoating tannin. The astringency is reinforced by a forbidding acidity, and as if that were not enough this is all within a fiery 13° + of alcohol. Nothing in the least blurred or hazy about that! Barbaresco, from a little further north and grown on a sandier soil is conventionally somewhat lighter and earlier to mature than Barolo. With wines made by the same producer this is often the case; between producers the distinction is rarely so clear.

When very young, Nebbiolo wines smell strongly of ripe cherries, plums and violets, but after only three or four years (with a minimum of two in wood for Barolo, one for Barbaresco) the fruity character changes dramatically and the nose becomes burnt, tarry, roasted with hints of oil, truffles and smoke.

Bizarre . . .? Yes. And true! The flavour of the wine changes in much the same way. The "fruity" character of the young wine is rarely part of the mature Barolo or Barbaresco experience because they take so long to soften. With such a distinctive constitution it might seem impossible to confuse a Nebbiolo wine with any other; but Syrah from the northern Rhône will oblige occasionally, as will Sangiovese based wines from Tuscany or even the odd Châteauneuf-du-Pape. Syrah has the tannin and acidity but a very different flavour and it takes much longer to brown in colour. One of the features which often marks a Nebbiolo wine is that, like Châteauneuf's Grenache, Chianti's Sangiovese and indeed Merlot, it turns brown fairly quickly, often displaying an orange rim after only four or five years. Chianti, however, is generally much paler, Châteauneuf much lower in acidity; and both are less drily astringent.

Styles vary considerably, but there is a general trend to vinify without stalks and to wood-age for a shorter period beyond the minimum in order to conserve the fruit more. Large old Slavonian chestnut or oak casks used to be the traditional ageing vessels, but new oak, if only as a small proportion, is making an appearance. (Gaja in Barbaresco especially.) The Co-operative wines from both Barolo and Barbaresco are excellent in a lighter style; other good producers are Pio Cesare, Ratti, Vietti, Conterno, Prunotto, Cordero, Cavallotto.

(**Left**) *One of the large old chestnut* botte, *(tuns), in which Barolo is traditionally aged. The legend on the board is a reminder that Barolo cannot be called such until it has spent a minimum of two years in cask. Until that time it is known as Nebbiolo da Barolo, or Nebbiolo for Barolo. This wine has also come from and been vinified as an individual vineyard, Bricco Sarras. It could be blended with the producer's other Barolo wines, or it could be bottled as a "Cru" wine, like an individual Burgundy vineyard.*

97

SANGIOVESE

Sangiovese is Tuscany's leading red wine grape, and Chianti its principal wine. Both have recently had something of an identity problem. The grape's two main clones, Sangiovese di Romagna and Sangioveto, produce wines of very different quality; the Sangioveto's being considerably better than the Romagna's bland offerings; but it was the latter that was extensively planted during the sixties and seventies. It is also only since 1984, when the rules of Chianti's new, elevated DOCG (Denominazione di Origine Controllata Garantita) status came into force, that the white grape component (usually the dull Trebbiano) has been reduced to a 2 per cent minimum and the almost equally neutral red Cannaiolo's to 5 per cent. At the same time the proportion of "other grapes" permitted was raised from 5 to 10 per cent – in effect meaning that more Cabernet Sauvignon could be added! The point is that prior to 1984 the proportion of Sangiovese could have been as low as 50 per cent (now 75 per cent), and what with the 15 per cent of wine or must from outside Chianti that could also have been added to the wine (now forbidden), it is not surprising that Chianti's and Sangiovese's style and quality have been so difficult to pinpoint.

There is no such animal as a "typical" Chianti or Chianti Classico. In addition to the variables I have already mentioned are those of whether or not to include Cabernet Sauvignon, whether or not to use Governo (qv), how long to age for in wood and in what kind of wood, etc. You may be forgiven for wondering if Sangiovese and Chianti can have any identifiable personality whatsoever after all that! But if you try a range of reputable producers' wines you should find some common threads.

Chianti is a medium bodied wine that is rarely very dark in colour, whose youthful purple-red rapidly turns brown. At four or five years its rim will already look brick coloured. The nose is usually fairly light and is a mixture of fragrant sweetness (roses), dry or cold tea and an impression of oiliness. Sounds very odd doesn't it, but my Chianti notes are full of "dry tea, sweet and oily" references. Although much less tannic than Nebbiolo wines there is also much less extract and flavour to mask the tannin. The wines are not so much tough as drily astringent, a lean texture which is reinforced by high acidity.

For good quality traditional Chiantis try those of Castello di Volpaia, Badia a Coltibuono or Castellare; and make a point of tasting Antinori's Chianti Classico to appreciate the way in which even a small percentage of Cabernet Sauvignon can noticeably enrich both bouquet and palate.

Pure, unalloyed Sangiovese does exist in Tuscany although it is a somewhat rarer wine, not to say more expensive: Brunello di Montalcino. Brunello is the name for the local Sangioveto (= Sangiovese Grosso) clone. By itself it makes a darker, more concentrated wine with some of the tarry, almost liquorice flavours and smoky aftertaste that might lead you to think it was a Nebbiolo wine. Failing the costly Biondi-Santi wines which need decades to mellow, try those of Altesino or Castelgiocondo; they are refined, complex and approachable. Rosso di Montalcinos are often "second wines" in effect, made from younger vines and with less wood age.

(**Below**) *The soft, warm tones of Tuscany at San Gimigniano, central Italy.*

TEMPRANILLO

Tempranillo is generally thought of as "the" grape of Rioja, although the wine is never made solely from this variety. That is one reason why it is difficult to say just what the grape is like. More significant though is that its grape flavours are always masked by the all embracing easy-please-easy-pall sweet vanilla of American oak. You can taste the grape unblended in the red wines from the Ribera del Duero (northwest Spain) where it is called the Tinto Fino. But you still cannot taste it unoaked. Here the mature Peñalba Lopez wines show it as slightly sweet, rather bland and fairly soft. Perhaps it needs the oak! On the other hand the Pesquera of Alejandro Fernandez, also made almost entirely from Tinto Fino, shows that with long maceration (over three weeks) you can make a wine of more personality from Tempranillo. It has been compared in style and quality to Petrus. This makes little sense; it is a good wine: tannic, oaky, quite complex and with an element of exotic spice; it is not "great" wine.

The pale brick red of mature Rioja is often a giveaway in a line up of red wines, but its sweet nose and flavour and light tannin have led many a blind taster to think it is a mature Burgundy from the Côte de Beaune.

GRENACHE

According to Jan Read the Garnacho Tinto, to call it by its Spanish name, originated in Aragon. Today in Spain it is best known as one of the grapes in the Rioja blend, where it is used to bolster the softness of Tempranillo. However, as it rarely accounts for more than 20 per cent of the recipe, and because the oak is going to get in the way, Rioja will not give you a good idea of what Grenache tastes and smells like. For that you need to move from its country of birth to its spiritual home: the Rhône Valley in southeast France. Here, in Côtes du Rhône or (better) Côtes du Rhône Villages, Gigondas, and Châteauneuf-du-Pape you will have wines based on up to two thirds Grenache and no new oak. Tavel rosé will contain the highest proportion of the grape but as a rosé you will notice the alcohol, rather than the flavour. Grenache's most obvious characteristic is high alcohol. Its bouquet is often unremarkable although the best have a sweet, jammy smell; hinting sometimes at aniseed or liquorice, and there is almost always an accompanying pep-

periness. In mature Châteauneufs there can be an attractive strawberry and roses sweetness mingled with a slightly farmyardy bouquet.

A higher proportion of Syrah in the blend (it is usually between 5 and 15 per cent) will make for a darker, stronger and more tannic wine, for Grenache is moderately coloured, quick to brown, relatively low in acidity and tannin. A modest Côtes du Rhône will be a full but flowing wine with a light earth and pepper fruit; Gigondas is generally chunkier, thicker textured and more tannic. Châteauneuf-du-Pape is always warm, generous and mouthfilling from its alcohol with a noticeably "sweet" fruit and a softish texture. Look as well for the distinctly hot, peppery finish.

> For proof that pure Grenache can, occasionally, make great wine, try Château Rayas from Châteauneuf. And compare a Gigondas or a Châteauneuf with a Crozes-Hermitage or Hermitage and notice how much broader, softer, sweeter and more generous the southern Rhônes feel compared to the pure Syrah wines which are darker in colour, more roasted and aromatic on the nose; less sweet but more concentrated and fiery on the palate, altogether sterner and more elegant.

(**Above**) *M. Reynaud of Château Rayas, Châteauneuf du Pape. A rather forbidding exterior lends credence to all those stories about his antisocial nature, but when he smiles his whole personality warms and softens and welcomes. His chaotic office and cobwebbed cellars are proof that you don't have to have stainless steel and computer programming to produce something special. The dusty barrels have pristine insides and harbour one of France's great red wines.*

GAMAY

Young Gamay (for which, read young Beaujolais) is a wine where one feels the colour description "purple" is not quite right. It has a distinctly blue tinge, making "violet" more appropriate. Its nose is a smooth blend of strawberry and bubble gum, and on the better quality wines I often find a hint of earth or chalkiness, occasionally even a light peppery character (the granite soil?).

On the palate most Beaujolais have very little tan

(**Right**) Gamay grapes in Beaujolais. Small compact bunches and an almost black colour suggest they would yield a much more substantial wine than most Beaujolais. (**Below**) Ridge Winery, south of San Francisco in California. Ridge specializes in Zinfandel and their wines show just how exciting and satisfying this grape can be.

nin so they can afford, indeed need, plenty of acidity to give them shape and thirstquenching appeal. Their flavour emphasis is on simple, juicy fruit and a smooth but refreshing feel (they are almost always best drunk cool, like white wine which is effectively what their structure is). These wines are not supposed to be complicated, just "moreish". The Beaujolais slang for them is "gouleyant", literally "gulpable".

Gamays grown elsewhere (very little outside France) rarely have the sleek, slip-down quality of Beaujolais. There are a few good ones from the Loire amongst many more that are just thin and sharp; but the nearer they are to Beaujolais itself the better they seem, witness those from the Côte Roannaise and Côtes du Forez, just west of Lyon.

Of the Beaujolais "Crus", the ten villages producing superior quality wine in the northern half of the Beaujolais region, Chiroubles is often the lightest and prettiest of all, Morgon and Moulin-à-Vent the most solid. Concentrated vintages of Moulin-à-Vent can age to resemble mature Pinot Noir from Burgundy, but that is hardly the point of Beaujolais and the Pinot it resembles is usually rather anonymous. Fleurie often appears to be the particularly fragrant or "flowery", although a lot of this may well be the suggestion of its undeniably pretty name.

ZINFANDEL

Zinfandel is California's grape. More interesting than the fact that its vinous progeny ranges from pale "blush" to thick, sweet Port-like wines, is that it makes really fine, characterful dry reds. This style of wine is deep purple with a briary, burnt-blackcurrant nose and a warm brambly, spicy flavour. It has a noticeably lively acidity, moderate tannin and can be remarkably complex. It is closest to northern Rhône Syrah perhaps in its spicy ripeness and firm acidity, but it is less tannic and doesn't have the smoky, minerally character of a northern Rhône. Heitz and Phelps make good examples in the Napa Valley, Calera and Ridge south of San Francisco. Zinfandel is something of a speciality at Ridge, and a comparison of its "Zins" from Napa (York Creek), San Luis Obispo (Paso Robles) and Amador County (Shenandoah and Fiddletown) is as rewarding as any of Cru Classé claret or individual vineyard Burgundies. In Western Australia Cape Mentelle makes a particularly good dry and savoury Zinfandel, but the grape is still fairly rare outside California.

ADDITIONAL RED GRAPE VARIETIES

DOLCETTO

A kind of Piedmontese gulper. The "dolce" of the name refers to its plummy fruit; it is not exactly "sweet". DOC Dolcettos are generous, mellow, but youthfully lively wines, with a low acidity by Piedmont grape standards (Nebbiolo and Barbera), modest tannin, and often a little carbon dioxide prickle. All to drink young, within two to three years.

BARBERA

Widely grown in Italy, but best known in the northwest. In common with Dolcetto it has little tannin, in contrast to Dolcetto it has a pronounced acidity. The wines have a mouthwatering combination of juicy, cherry rich fruit and vigorous acidity. The spectrum runs from straightforward and fruity (Fontanafredda) to dense, oak-aged wines of very good quality (Barbera d'Alba of Renato Ratti and Gaja).

CORVINA

Mainly from northeast Italy, the principal grape in the blend making up Valpolicella and Bardolino, and which provides the finesse. Styles run from light, crimson coloured and sharp-but-fluid cherry fruit wines, to the almost Port-like, sweet Recioto della Valpolicella. A common theme is the smell and taste of cherrystones or almond kernel bitterness. Recioto della Valpolicella (semi-sweet) and Recioto della Valpolicella Amarone (dry) are both made from the ripest, selected grapes, partially dried. The Amarone (from Amaro, meaning bitter) is a strong (16° +), concentrated, velvety wine with a grape skin bitterness to nose and palate; a fiery but fine afterdinner wine to sip with nuts or strong cheeses. The sweet Recioto (14°–15°) is Port-like in that it is sweet and strong, but it is nothing like *as* sweet, nor *as* alcoholic (it is not fortified) and its bitter sweet flavour is unique. Remarkable and highly individual wines. Amongst the best are those of Masi, Tedeschi, Quintarelli, Allegrini.

MOURVÈDRE

The solid, tannic core to the wines of Bandol where it must now account for at least 50 per cent of the wine. Also used in Châteauneuf-du-Pape and Côtes du Rhône Villages where it is a robust backbone to Grenache and Cinsaut.

(**Left**) *"Barbera is found here". One of the many Piedmontese wine route signs, that look more helpful than they are.*

CINSAUT

Moderately tannic and with quite good acidity, mainly seen in wines from France's Midi. As its wine is often rather rustic and lacking in "centre", Cabernet or Syrah come to its aid for both core and character. South Africa's Pinotage grape is a crossing of Pinot and Cinsaut.

(**Above**) *The Tedeschi brothers; enthusiasts and experimenters, they make a wide range of characterful Valpolicellas and fine Soaves.*

CHAMPAGNE &
SPARKLING WINES

THE METHODS

Dom Pérignon . . . isn't he the French monk who invented Champagne? Dom Pérignon's name is familiar even to the teetotaller, and the context is champagne, although beyond that details may be rather hazy. He no more "invented" champagne than did the "widow" Clicquot, although they both contributed significantly to the development and consistent production of the style of drink we know today. Carbon dioxide bubbles are a natural part of the fermentation process and it seems likely that the origin of "sparkling" wines was as a result of unfinished fermentation in the region's cold climate.

Fermentation would have started after the harvest, stopped before completion as it became too cold at the onset of winter, and begun again the following spring, so producing a finished wine with noticeable residual fizz eight months or so later. It was the attractive texture that the bubbles gave to this wine that made them worth preserving, and it was Dom Pérignon, in the late seventeenth century, who was the first to make a careful study of how best to do this, and who used cork, and later the stronger English glass (*verre anglais*) as the solution. At least as important was his perfection of the art of blending different wines, and his improving on the method of pressing *black* grapes rapidly in order to obtain a *white* wine; for champagne is a blended wine, produced from white and black grapes. In Dom Perignon's time the amount of sparkle in the wines would have been variable and a matter of chance. The means of con-

(**Right**) *Pinot Noir grapes (plus a rogue albino bunch) being distributed round a traditional Champagne press.* (**Below right**) *This series of pictures of the juice pressed from the Pinot Noir clearly shows the rosy hue that the must has to begin with. Most of this will be lost during fermentation and ageing, but it does seem to give Champagnes from white and red grapes a deeper yellow (occasionally salmon) cast than those made from Chardonnay alone.*

sistently producing a calculated amount of sparkle were not developed until well into the eighteenth century. This was the Champagne Method (*méthode champenoise*) as we know it today.

CHAMPAGNE METHOD (méthode champenoise)

First fermentation The base wines are made, separately, from three principal grape varieties: the white Chardonnay, and the red Pinot Noir and Pinot Meunier. Today fermentation is rarely in oak barrels, instead temperature controlled stainless steel vats are the most common method used (Krug and Alfred Gratien still ferment entirely in oak, Bollinger partly).

Assemblage In the following spring these wines, and possibly others from stock, are blended to the house styles. This is the dry white wine which will undergo a second fermentation in bottle.

Second fermentation A measured quantity of sugar and yeast is added to the still wine which is then bottled and sealed with a crown cap. The amount of sugar, fermented by the yeast, will increase the alcoholic content by just over 1° and produce a pressure of 75lbs per square inch, three times the pressure in an average car tyre! The second fermentation and creation of the sparkle will be largely finished within a fortnight but by law the wine must remain in contact with the yeast for a minimum period of two months before the lees are removed.

Riddling If the deposit created by the second fermentation were not removed from the bottle, the wine would become horribly cloudy upon opening. It was Madame Clicquot who invented the method for encouraging the sediment in the bottle to settle on the inverted cork, or nowadays a small plastic pot under the crown cap. Her original, labour intensive method, has been superceded, but not entirely

(**Far left, top**) *A clear bottle reveals the yeast sediment resulting from the second fermentation in bottle.*
(**Near left**) *Riddling, either by hand, as here, or mechanically, is a process of encouraging all this deposit to settle on the end of the inverted cork (**far left, centre**). The bottle is upended from the horizontal position over a period of weeks by a series of gradual "twist and lift" movements. The white indicators on the bottom of the bottles help the riddler judge his "eighth of a turn".*
(**Far left, bottom**) *Even today the occasional bottle bursts before riddling takes place, leaving just a layer of dead yeast; Krug yeast no less!*

replaced, by more modern mechanical systems.

Ageing on lees Before disgorgement takes place, the champagne's quality can be considerably enhanced if it is left in contact with its yeast lees. This period of ageing allows the wine to pick up the subtle yeasty character that is the hallmark of fine young champagnes; a character which takes on a more biscuity nuance with age. In the case of cheaper wines this period will only be a few months, in the case of expensive wines it may be several years.

Disgorgement The neck of the inverted bottle is immersed two to three inches deep in a sub zero solution for up to twenty minutes, partly freezing the liquid in the neck. This slushy plug prevents the yeast sediment from falling back into the wine when the bottle is turned upright. As the crown cap is then removed the plug is cleanly ejected by the gas pressure and with it the sediment.

Dosage and corking Still wine "dosed" with cane sugar to produce the required degree of dryness or sweetness is used to top up the bottle before corking and wiring.

OTHER METHODS OF CREATING THE SPARKLE

Sparkling wines made by the following two methods have a fizz which is larger bubbled, coarser in texture and more explosive on the palate; it is also much more short lived.

Tank Method In this case the second fermentation takes place in large pressurized tanks to which the yeast and sugar have been added. The sparkling wine is filtered and bottled, under pressure, directly from these tanks.

Carbonation The cheapest method of all. Here the wine is brought to below freezing point in a large tank, the carbon dioxide is injected and the wine bottled under pressure.

*(**Above**) Inverted Champagne bottles with their necks in a freezing saline solution. 20 minutes or so in this position will produce a slushy plug of ice (**opposite top**) imprisoning the yeast sediment.*

*(**Right**) Bottles of Krug in February 1985. 580 bottles laid down for their second fermentation (in bottle) in April 1980 and untouched thereafter. The longer they remain thus the more subtle flavours they will pick up from the yeast deposit, and the mellower they will become. They will also cost more!*

CHILLING AND OPENING SPARKLING WINES

If, like me, you rarely plan your champagne or sparkling consumption well in advance, there is no harm whatsoever in chilling it rapidly in the freezer. The only conceivable hazard is forgetting it is there. Ten to twenty minutes is adequate, or until it feels cool enough to the touch. Apart from the freshening appeal of chilled white wine, the cooler the temperature, the more slowly the mousse (sparkle) will be released.

And how do you stop the wine bubbling over on opening? Ease the cork from the bottle while holding it at about 30° from the horizontal (it is often easier to turn the bottle by its base, rather than the cork) – the principle is the same, in reverse, as pouring beer into a nearly horizontal glass to avoid a head. When filling your champagne flute you can either fill at a slant, as with beer, or else pour a little into each glass first, allow the froth to die down and then top up.

TASTING SPARKLING WINE

The problem is that the fizz gets in the way! Bouquet, flavour, development on the palate and length of aftertaste are important as for all wines, but the texture of the mousse is the individual key to quality here. In wines made by the champagne method, the bubbles are not only smaller, thus finer and "creamier" in feel, but they are more closely combined with other components in the liquid. For this reason they come out of solution less rapidly, the mousse is less aggressive to the palate and lasts longer. This quality is also enhanced the longer the wine has been left to age on its lees before disgorgement.

CHAMPAGNE

Champagne is made principally from three grape varieties, Chardonnay, Pinot Noir and Pinot Meunier; proportions vary considerably in different wines. Pinot Noir accounts for roughly one-third of the vines throughout the region, but there is considerably more Chardonnay than Pinot Meunier in the top quality vineyards (Grand and Premier Cru). Chardonnay is what provides champagne with its elegance, finesse and backbone, and in particular the ability to age gracefully. Comparing a "Blanc de Blancs" (pure Chardonnay) with a standard champagne will show the Chardonnay wine as leaner but more refined. Good wines to try are Deutz, Pol Roger Cuvée de Blancs and, more expensive but superb, Taittinger Comtes de Champagne Blanc de Blancs.

Pinot Noir provides a champagne with more breadth and depth of fruit, a bit more roundness and "cushion" (Serena Sutcliffe's evocative word). By itself it soon becomes ponderous and makes one wish for more of the freshness and definition given by Chardonnay. Pinot Meunier, the other black grape, makes a less distinguished wine than either Pinot Noir or Chardonnay; it has plenty of fruit but not a great deal of interest or length. Its advantage is that it is easier to grow and serves to fill out less expensive champagnes that will be drunk relatively early. "Blanc de Noirs" wines (white wines from only black grapes) are rare.

Although champagne is a "white" wine, the red grapes that are used for it will often reveal its identity in a line up of sparklers. Assuming it is not a Blanc de Blancs its colour will usually have a pinkish cast. Truly pink "rosé" champagnes can be made either by blending red and white wines or by permitting a limited maceration on the skins; I find many of them have a light but unwelcome astringency.

(**Left top**) *The slushy ice plug retaining the yeast sediment, just before disgorgement.* (**Below left**) *Disgorgement by hand. Traditional disgorgement by hand is without the ice plug! Today, the crown cap is normally removed, the champagne "dosed" and the bottle immediately corked, all in one automatic operation.*

(**Opposite, below**) *Champagne corks achieve their compressed shape progressively the longer they are in the bottle, changing from a vague "waist" (second from the left), through varying degrees of "skirt" to a polished cylinder (**far right**). This tells you how long it is since the Champagne was disgorged and corked. In the case of non vintage Champagnes this gives a useful indication of how much "bottle age" the wine has. A shape like that second from the left indicates very little bottle age since corking, and if the wine is rather green it would improve, by softening, with another six to twelve months ageing. Its cork would then look more like the third or fourth from the left.*

Mousse is the feature that gives sparkling wines their appeal, and the texture quality of that mousse is one of the best ways of assessing the wines. Apart from bouquet, flavour and length, the finer and "creamier" the feel of the bubbles, and the longer they last, both in the glass and on the palate, the better the quality the wine is likely to be. A fine texture allows you to taste the other components of the wine as well; less distinguished wines have larger, coarser bubbles which are explosive as soon as you sip them, making it difficult to perceive anything else; they also usually disappear with the suddenness that they burst on the palate initially.

To experience a really fine texture try a top notch champagne such as Dom Pérignon or Roederer Crystal, both vintage wines; for a non-vintage (NV) example Ayala is often a good bet. If possible, for comparison, taste it next to a Cava from Spain, or a sparkler from California or Australia. And to feel the effect of wood on champagne texture and flavour, try Krug NV for a delicate oak nuttiness, and Bollinger NV for a rather more open-grained, sometimes coarser (some would say characterful) feel; Roederer Brut Premier is another non-vintage wine where you can detect the agreeable influence of "wood as added complexity". All of these have a little "pull" on the gums from the wood tannin.

(**Below**) *The Côte des Blancs, south of Epernay in Champagne, looking east to the village of Le Mesnil. This "côte" is planted almost exclusively with Chardonnay, hence its name.*

(**Right**) *The characteristic Champagne soil profile: a profound complex of pure chalk under 30 cm (12 in) or so of cultivated topsoil.*

SPARKLING WINES

France has many other sparkling wines which make for useful comparisons with champagne. Sparkling Vouvray, Saumur Mousseux or Crémant de Loire, Crémant d'Alsace, Crémant de Bourgogne and Blanquette de Limoux. These are all champagne method wines. Ackermann Laurence is very reliable from Saumur, Langlois Château makes really stylish and classy Loire sparklers not surprisingly perhaps as it is owned by Bollinger. Langlois Crémant Rosé is particularly successful. Look for the telltale earthy/chalky smell and flavour of Cabernet Franc, one of the principal red varieties used in the Loire sparklers from Saumur. Blanquette de Limoux, (from the south of France, near Carcassonne) is usually light, dry and fresh, and, dare I say it, quite possible to confuse with lesser non-vintage champagne blind. Clairette de Die Tradition (from the Rhône) is the Clairette to try; it is often pétillant (slightly sparkling) rather than sparkling, and tastes distinctly of the finer Muscat grape.

Crémant de Bourgogne can be very good, particularly from Mâcon where it has a high proportion of Chardonnay (the Viré or Lugny Cooperative wines are excellent), with the whites being much more successful than the rosés. Crémant d'Alsace is generally less distinctive than the Loire or Burgundy examples.

Cava (champagne method) wines from Spain are good if without much finesse, but neither are they expensive! I usually find their bouquet rather earthy/minerally, sometimes with a slightly rubbery character too. On the palate they are rarely very dry, generally softish, with the earthy flavour smelled on the nose and a distinctly soft, warm finish. An additional giveaway on the lesser ones is the coarse attack of the mousse. Freixenet Black Label is one of the finest, and Raimat's Chardonnay sparkler is also excellent.

German Sekt is usually pretty unremarkable, even when it is not green-apple dry, but do try Deinhard Lila which is delicious, if hardly representative; a gently sparkling, off-dry wine with a distinct mature Riesling nose and flavour.

The majority of good Italian sparklers are Asti Spumante, but there are some surprisingly successful champagne lookalikes from Ca' del Bosco in Lombardy.

Notable sparklers from California are from the Russian River Basin: Sonoma Vineyard and Iron Horse, the latter is one of the best. Schramsberg is perhaps the best known, and although they are wines of some finesse, I often find the bubbles too "foamy" to be able to get at the flavours easily, especially when young. And whereas age mellows them it seems to lose their fruit length as well.

Australian champagne method wines come mainly from Victoria; Seppelt is the most complete, Château Remy, Taltarni, Mildara and Yellowglen some of the other better known ones. On the whole they are good frothy sparklers, frequently with the telltale lime and lemon flavours. Tyrrell and Rosemount now make more expensive versions in New South Wales.

Even India makes a very respectable champagne method Chardonnay – Omar Khayyam.

(**Left**) The main feature of champagne, or indeed any sparkling wine, is its bubbles and there is something distinctly dampening about not being able to see that the wine is sparkling. Contemplating the rising mousse is very much part of the appeal and this is best observed in tall glasses or ones with a hollow stem.

The same champagne will froth differently in different glasses as the CO_2 requires a flawed surface to set it free. Glasses with the smoothest, most perfect inner surface will yield very little bubble at all as the illustration shows. One occasionally comes across champagne glasses which have had a small section of their bottom inner surface roughened with a diamond drill . . . not a bad idea.

From left to right: late 19th century English or French (the pattern was produced on both sides of the Channel); a flute from the modern "Classic" range made in Bohemia; an early 20th century German flute; and a modern French stemless glass which is as exhilarating to look at as to drink from.

FORTIFIED WINES

Fortification is the addition of alcohol, usually in the form of neutral grape brandy, to part fermented or fully fermented wine. It is added to *partly fermented wine* in order to halt the fermentation and so preserve a degree of natural sweetness as in Port, sweet Madeiras and French Vin Doux Naturel (V.D.N.) for example. It is added to *fully fermented wine* in order to make it more robust and prevent spoilage during ageing and transport, Sherry being the best known wine of this type.

Of these Sherry was probably the earliest to be fortified. The "Sack" of Shakespeare's day was a fortified wine, but Madeira was not regularly fortified until the mid-eighteenth century, Port not until the mid-nineteenth century, by when it had been discovered, in each case, that with time the fortified wines developed into something much more interesting than the original unfortified product.

SHERRY

All sherries start as dry white wines of anywhere between 11° and 14°. After fermentation is complete they are classified into two broad categories; *Fino* and *Oloroso*. The Fino wines are lighter and will develop into "Fino" and "Amontillado" styles, the Olorosos are heavier, destined to become "Oloroso", "Cream" and "Brown" sherries. As a result of this initial classification the Fino wines are fortified to 15.5°, the optimum degree for the growth of *Flor*, and the Olorosos are fortified to 18°.

Flor A "surface" yeast, indigenous to the Sherry region, which develops spontaneously, forming a crinkly white skin on the surface of the wine. As a skin it protects the sherry from oxygen; at the same time it feeds on any traces of residual sugar and glycerine, and creates additional aldehydes and esters, so imparting the bone dry taste and particular nose of Fino.

The solera system Sherry left to mature on its own develops haphazardly, hardly a suitable basis for commerce, and the point of the solera system is to ensure a consistency of style and quality. Its principle is that of controlled blending, where young fortified wine added slowly to older wine will take on the characteristics of the older wine. A solera stock will consist of wines in casks of varying ages, roughly a year apart. As the older wines are drawn off for blending into the final brands, so the casks are topped up with younger wines. The system relies on not more than a third of a cask being withdrawn per year.

(**Right**) *Sherry butts showing marks that are chalked onto the barrels of young wines when they are first classified into the lighter "fino" or fuller "oloroso" styles. The category will determine the wine's future treatment and development. Individual markings vary from one bodega to another.*

Blending The final stage in the making of Sherry. Blending replicates existing styles or brands. All Finos will remain dry, as will most Amontillados and the pure Olorosos. Sweetened sherries are based on Olorosos though, varying according to the amounts of sweet wines blended in. The latter are high quality mistellas (qv) made from Pedro Ximenez or Muscatel grapes; both are rich, concentrated and intensely sweet, and themselves drawn from soleras of varying ages. The quality of any Sherry will depend finally on the proportion of old wine in the blend.

Styles

Finos Because they are protected by flor, Finos are subject to minimal oxydation and are therefore very pale in colour – usually a pale straw. Manzanilla is the lightest Fino of all (about 16°) and is bone dry with a distinct piquancy and salty tang to it, said to come from its being aged near the sea at Sanlucar de Barrameda. Standard Finos are a little fuller, dry, but with less bite than Manzanilla; both have the distinctive flor nose which is a faintly nutty pungency, occasionally suggestive of the yeast itself. Manzanillas are quite rare and need to be drunk young as do all Finos. Domecq "La Ina", Garvey "San Patricio" and Gonzalez Byass "Tio Pepe" are good examples, Gonzalez' "Elegante" is a very slightly sweetened Fino.

Amontillado These wines have Fino parentage, but only a year or two under flor, so they are lightly oxydized and consequently darker, usually amber or tawny in colour. Longer exposure to oxygen also gives them a more "rancio" nose, a distinctly buttery (but not rancid) nuttiness. These are a fuller Fino style. "Commercial" examples may not be dry, but some of the very finest sherries are old dry Amontillados, pungently nutty wines with wonderfully penetrating flavours, rich and concentrated but also fiercely dry. Barbadillo's "Principe", Valdespinos' "Don Tomas" and Gonzalez Byass' "Amontillado del Duque" are such wines.

Palo Cortado I am not at all sure just what this animal is – and to judge by the variety of styles under that name, nor are the shippers! The theory is that it is a wine which develops neither as an Amontillado nor as an Oloroso, but somewhere in between with the flavoury cut of the first, the fullness and fragrance of the second. Valdespino's "Cardinal" is at any rate a supremely elegant example of these rare wines.

Oloroso Dry Olorosos are difficult to distinguish from dry Amontillados but in general an Oloroso will be darker, amber to brown, and a softer wine with a particularly fragrant character on nose and finish.

(Oloroso in Spanish means fragrant.) Williams and Humbert's "Dos Cortados" shows this combination of rich dry flavour and soft fragrance, a superb wine. The sweetened Olorosos also have this softer roundness and perfumed character. Good ones to try are Sandeman's "Royal Corregidor", Gonzalez Byass' "Apostoles" (medium sweet) and "Matusalem" – caramel and butter concentration.

Almacenista Sherries Almacenistas are people who store and age small stocks of very fine, unblended sherries. These are sometimes bought by the large merchant houses for blending, and they are also occasionally marketed on their own (Emilio Lustau especially).

Montilla-Moriles From the Andalucian hills behind Malaga, Montilla-Moriles is not really a fortified wine as the Pedro Ximenez grapes easily ripen to 14° and more in what are some of the hottest vineyards in Spain. In comparison with Sherry, Montilla's distinctive feature is its lower alcohol and softer feel. Taste a dry Montilla next to a Fino Sherry and the difference in style will be very clear.

MARSALA

My image of Sicily's Marsala was for a long time of a coarse, sweet, burnt caramel flavoured wine mainly used to flavour Italian desserts. And there is plenty of that kind of Marsala to be had. But look instead for the dry "Vergine", a refined, savoury, fragrant wine, rather like a light, pale Oloroso Sherry. Two of the best names for Marsala are de Bartoli (Vecchio Samperi), and Rallo (Old Label 1860).

(**Above**) *Inside a barrel, showing the surface yeast "flor" on a Fino sherry, looking just like fresh cream cheese. It is flor which gives Fino sherry its particular bouquet and bone dry flavour.*

PORT

Port is fortified during fermentation so that it retains a considerable degree of sweetness. Once the must has reached between 5°–6° it is run off into large vats filled to one fifth with grape brandy at 77°, stopping any further fermentation. As the must ferments for a comparatively short period, there is limited contact with the skins and pips so that the "extraction" process must be accelerated if there is to be sufficient colour and tannin.

This used to be achieved by treading the grapes in a lagar, but as this is so labour intensive it is now reserved for only the very best grapes. Instead auto-vinifiers are used which are more practical, more efficient and cheaper.

Styles of Port These vary according to three factors: (1) whether the wine is "dated" or not: Vintage Port, Port with a harvest date and Ports with an Indicated Age are "dated". (2) Whether the wine matures in cask or bottle or both. Most Port matures in wood, hence the generic name "wood port". Vintage Port is the only one to mature solely in bottle. (3) Whether the wine is from a single harvest, or a blend of years. Most Port is a blended wine, only Vintage, Late Bottled Vintage and those with a harvest date come from a single vintage, and these account for only a small proportion of the Port trade.

Ruby and Tawny ports are blended to a house style, and after three or four years in wood they should be fresh and fruity-sweet; one can't expect much more from them.

Old Tawny is the finest of the "wood" ports. It frequently betrays its red grape origin by having a distinct reddish or mahogany cast in its colour (particularly noticeable when compared with the olive or tawny gold of a Sercial Madeira for example) and it varies from an almost ruby hue to a pale, true tawny. The longer these wines spend in wood the lighter and more polished they become, whilst their flavour concentrates and becomes more complex. Look for a delicate woodiness on the nose; a fine texture, a mellow

(**Above right**) *Modern Port vinification. Gently fermenting carmine must in an autovinifier, gathering in the reservoir above the vat. After a gasping release of pressure in the latter the must will flood back into the vat under its own weight, bruising the skins and doing the work of colour and tannin extraction previously done by men's feet. The build up of pressure from fermentation gases will then start to force the liquid back into the upper reservoir once more, and so the cycles continue.*

(**Right**) *Old fashioned vinification. Port must, thick and grainy with skins and pips, pours into a cement lagar where it will be trodden to extract the maximum colour and tannin during the brief period of fermentation on the skins, before it is run off and fortified.*

caramel and butter sweetness. At 20 and 40 years old they can have an almost liqueur like smoothness and a wonderful lacy delicacy about them. Port's finest, along with the Vintage wines. Warre's "Nimrod" is always very good, Noval and Taylor's 20- and 40-year-olds are the cream of the old tawnies.

Late Bottled Vintage (LBV) traditionally spent four years in wood before being bottled, and therefore still had deposit to throw and still needed cellaring for a further three or four years. They were good quality wines from lesser vintages. Were, because most LBV today is bottled after six years in cask, plus filtering. It is Port's fastest growing market and the wines are now light and peppery-sweet and bear little resemblance to Vintage Port.

Crusted Port So called because it throws a "crust" (deposit) in bottle, Not (yet) recognized in Portugal. A blend of vintages shipped in bulk and bottled in the United Kingdom, and requiring two to four years cellaring thereafter. Lighter "Vintage" style.

Single Quinta Vintage ports from lighter years, from the vineyards of the shipper's best "farms" (quintas). These are the backbone of the Vintage Ports but never as complete by themselves. They have all the characteristics of Vintage Port but in a less grand manner. Taylor's "Vargellas" and Fonseca's "Guimaraens" (a brand) are very reliable.

Vintage Port "Declared" only in the best vintages if they are considered good enough after a couple of years in barrel. The very best of what port has to offer, blended from a variety of vineyards. Lighter vintages need 10 to 15 years (1975, 1980, 1982) others (1963, 1966, 1970, 1977, 1983, 1985) nearer 20 to mellow and harmonize. When mature they should have a sweet and penetrating bouquet (raisins, liquorice, dried figs), peppery richness still with some fire in it, complexity and length. And if they don't you have every right to be disappointed, particularly if the wine is from one of the top houses: Taylor, Graham, Fonseca, Warre, Dow or Noval. Taylor, the most famous of them all, is generally referred to as the "Latour" of Ports, referring not only to its quality but especially to its weight, concentration and power. Since the 1966 vintage I think "Lafite" might be a better comparison as in my experience it has never been the sweetest (usually Graham) nor the most concentrated (variously Fonseca, Warre or Dow) but it has always been the most perfumed, elegant and refined. I think to look for a "Latour" is to be regularly disappointed. Perhaps the moral is not to make the comparison at all!

> Compare if you can, a basic Tawny with Warre's "Nimrod" and a 20 or 40 year old; and a basic Ruby with an LBV and a (relatively) mature Vintage or Single Quinta. The same shipper would show the differences more clearly.

Tasting Port In much the same way that tasting sparkling wine is more difficult because the bubbles get in the way, tasting Port at 20°–21°, especially immature Vintage Port, has the problem of the spirit blurring the subtleties and making them more difficult to perceive. The impact of tannin is considerably lessened because of the wines' sweetness. What one doesn't want in any Port is an obvious taste of raw "spirit", on the palate or on the finish. Whatever type of Port, the concentration of flavour and sugar should mask (ie balance) the alcohol, so that one is not aware of it as such. In young Vintage Port one can taste the raw ingredients of sugar, alcohol and tannin as individual elements, and it takes years for them to harmonize so that you no longer notice them as separate. When the wine is in decline and the fruit is "drying out", then the spirit begins to "show" again, first as a "hot" finish, finally as a burn on the palate.

In contrast to Sherry or Madeira, most Port has a touch of pepper on the nose, and a minerally character under its sweetness on the palate.

A port "pipe", the local name for a barrel containing approximately 56 dozen bottles. Gone are the days when generous godfathers laid down pipes of Port for their godchildren. Generosity comes in cases of one dozen today!

*Estufas, literally hot
houses, may be heated rooms
with casks in them for the
finer wines, or enormous vats
heated by coils for the others.
The wine is heated to between
40°–50°C (105°–125°F) for a
minimum of three months,
although it can be much
longer. After a slow cooling
period the wines are stored in
lots according to quality and
type, and it is from this store
of wines, varying in age from
eighteen months to twenty
years and more, and in
quality from the ordinary to
the very finest, that Madeira
is blended. The only
unblended wines are* **vintage**
*madeiras, entirely from one
harvest and one grape variety.*

MADEIRA

The best known Madeiras are described by their
grape variety: Sercial, Verdelho, Bual and Malmsey.
The finest Madeiras will be made solely from these
varieties, but the lesser wines have, until recently,
contained only a proportion of their "name" grapes,
and have been blended instead to the degree of
sweetness typical of the grape type: Sercial being the
driest although never bone dry, Verdelho off-dry,
Bual medium-sweet, and Malmsey intensely sweet.

The fortification of Madeira is a much more flexible
affair than that of Sherry or Port. The *finer* wines are
fortified during fermentation when there is the appropriate amount of residual sugar according to their
grape. The *lesser* wines are fermented dry, sweetened
according to type with "surdo" (a mistella similar to
Germany's süssreserve), and fortifed after going
through "estufa" (qv). The wines then undergo a
period of estufa, or heating, a process exclusive to
Madeira, and which bestows on the wine its unique
characteristics: vital acidity, caramelly flavour and
potential for longevity.

Estufa Estufa has a truly romantic origin. In the
eighteenth century Madeira was fortified prior to
shipment to the East Indies. Initially much of the wine
was simply loaded as ballast and so made the round

trip, being subjected to extremes of heat, in the
tropics, and cold round the southern cape. It was soon
discovered that these wines gained considerably from
the long voyages, and they began to be matured in
this way deliberately, subsequently being named after
the ships in which they had travelled. In the early part
of the nineteenth century merchants began to try and
reproduce the alternate conditions of heat and cold on
the island itself, leading to the development of the
modern estufa system.

There are two keys to Madeira; the first is its
acidity. The young wines are by nature piercingly tart
and this "cut" is never lost; always giving a superb
definition, a very clean, dry finish, and an extraordinary freshness even to wines that are decades and
sometimes centuries old. The second is the effect of
the estufa process on the taste. It produces a high
level of aldehydes which give the "rancio" butter and
nut character to the nose, as well as the typical
caramel or burnt-sugar taste to the palate. And these
two together allow the best wines to age and mellow
to a very special concentration and clarity of flavours.

If the "rancio" might lead to confusion with Sherry
on the nose, the acidity on the palate would certainly
not, nor would the underlying caramelly flavour. And
the pale gold, through amber to molasses brown

colours could never be Port.

Names and categories Before Madeira joined the European Common Market in 1986 it could call all its wines by the principal grape varieties (Sercial, Verdelho, Bual and Malmsey) whether the wines contained a high proportion of these grapes or not – and many *did* not. The grapes had become synonymous with a style at least as much as a grape variety, and a high proportion of the cheaper wines consisted of the workhorse Tinta Negra Mole grape more than anything else. As Madeira cannot change the make up of its vineyards overnight, and as over half the vines are still Negra Mole, it may continue to call its "under five year old" wines by a grape variety until 1992, after which they will have to describe the wines as dry, medium-dry, medium-sweet or rich, unless they contain at least 85 per cent of the named varietal. All the finer categories must already contain this statutory minimum of the "noble" grape variety named.

Classifications

Vintage From one harvest and 100 per cent one varietal. Have to be kept in cask for a minimum of 20 years, plus two in bottle before sale. They are not usually even "declared" for well over a quarter of a century!
Extra Reserve Blends with a minimum age of 15 years.
Special Reserve Blends with a minimum age of 10 years.
Reserve Blends with a minimum age of five years.
Finest, Choice, Selected Minimum age three years.
Soleras Madeira production is based on the solera system, but wines are sometimes sold as "dated" soleras, a system which is under review at present because of the difficulty of "keeping track" of, and verifying the wine's, year of origin. Bureaucracy rules!

Styles

Tinta Negra Mole You can recognize this variety in its youth, and in lesser Madeiras, by its very distinctive but undistinguished "cheesy" smell. Otherwise it is a chameleon, assuming whatever style is required by blending, but capable of producing fine (and no longer cheesy) mature wines in its own right.
Sercial Off dry, rarely bone dry; pale golden in colour; dry rancio nose; tangy, lemon edged flavour.
Verdelho Medium-dry, amber coloured; more buttery rancio nose; and dryish, caramel backed flavour.
Bual Medium-sweet to sweet; golden brown colour; smoky, fragrant, aromatic rancio; more buttery caramel sweetness often with a smoky aftertaste.
Malmsey Sweet and rich; nut to dark brown; deep, sweet, burnt caramel and nut flavour, reflecting a

similar bouquet.

These are the basic characteristics of each grape style. The best way to get to know them is obviously to taste the four next to each other at the same quality level and then, much more interesting, to compare the different quality levels. As they get older the basic style remains the same but the wines increase in intensity and concentration of flavour, but those flavours also develop for longer on the palate, they are crystal clear to perceive and they are sustained with great aromatic length on the finish.

> Particularly good wines of 10-year-old quality and above for comparison (and which are reasonably widely available) are:
> Sercial: Cossart Gordon "Duo Centenary"
> Verdelho: Lomelino "Superior Golden Verdelho"
> Bual: Cossart Gordon "Duo Centenary"
> Malmsey: Blandy's 10-year-old.
> Henriques and Henriques (vintages and old soleras in particular) and Rutherford and Miles are two other excellent producers.

Madeiras are such remarkable wines with so much to offer per sniff and sip, that if I had only *one* bottle that I could take with me to that desert island, it would not be the finest claret, or white Burgundy; not a great Sauternes, German Beerenauslese or Australian Liqueur Muscat, nor even a fine Barolo, Côte Rôtie or Hermitage; it would be a vintage Madeira, preferably Bual, and probably twice my age.

VIN DOUX NATUREL

See Muscat and Grenache.

(**Above**) *The island of Madeira is very small and very steep. Competition is fierce for usable land and the choice between "vine or brick" is often difficult. The pressure on existing vineyards has recently been exacerbated by the demand for hotels for tourists. It is not surprising then, to see the vine relegated to sites such as this precarious ledge, halfway down a cliff face, or to the almost inaccessible beach below. Bananas, just visible beyond the ledge, are further competition: bananas don't need spraying or pruning and they provide you with more than one crop a year!*

SPIRITS

DISTILLATION

Wine is nine-tenths water, and one-tenth alcohol and flavouring. Whisky or brandy are similar, but with a much lower proportion of water. The molecules of alcohol and water cling to each other whatever the concentration (unlike oil and water for example), but as their molecules become volatile and vapourize at different temperatures (alcohol "boils" at 78°C/173°F, water at 100°C/212°F) they can be separated by heating. An alcohol/water mixture heated at 79°C (175°F), will eventually vapourize *all* the alcohol but only *some* of the water; both will condense on cooler surfaces to produce a liquid with a much higher alcohol concentration. This is the essence of distillation.

Every other flavour and aroma constituent in a wine (or in the "wash" for Whisky) also has a different vaporization point, dependent on temperature and its rate of increase. This means that unpleasant fractions of the condensing liquids can be rejected as they appear: the highly volatile "heads" ("foreshots" in Whisky) early on, the low volatility "tails" ("feints" for Whisky) towards the end of the heating process. In deciding which fractions to include and which to reject lies the art of distillation.

COGNAC

Cognac is distilled twice in a pot still from thin, acid wine. The *first* distillation lasts eight-to-ten hours, reduces the wine by a third and produces a bland, watery spirit, milky in appearance and about 28° in strength. This is known as the "brouillis" (literally "brew"), the last third of which are the "tails", drawn off separately and put back into the next charge of wine. The *second* distillation, known as the "bonne chauffe" distills the brouillis. It lasts for 16 hours or so, reducing the brouillis by half, of which only half again is actually Cognac. The first few per cent of distillate are the "heads". These are intolerable to smell, causing an instant feeling of nausea; and they are potent, harsh, dry and acrid to taste. Collected separately they go back into the wine. The next fraction is the "coeur" or "heart", destined for Cognac. This results in a pure white spirit of about 68°; soft, sweet and surprisingly fruity in aroma; clean, pure and fiery on the palate. What is left produces roughly half "seconds", a weaker spirit, harsh, dull peppery, and which are added to the next brouillis; and half "tails", an unpleasant, watery coda: cooked, flat and bitter; destined, like the heads, for the next wine charge.

Maturation The new spirit spends its first year in new, open grained Limousin or Tronçais oak after

(**Margin**) *Distiller's aids: hydrometer and thermometer (**top**) indicate when a "cut" is approaching. Here the cut – at around 60° of alcohol – from "heart" to "seconds" is close; the stillman's nose is final arbiter. And, when the "seconds" are close to the "tails", they will develop a head of bubbles when shaken.* (**middle and bottom**).

which it is entitled to the Cognac appellation. After the first year it goes into older barrels to mature. Cognac gains colour, flavour and extra definition from the soluble substances in the wood: tannin, lignin, vanillin and sugars. It softens with a gentle oxydation, develops a more subtle, less fruity bouquet, and gradually concentrates by evaporation.

ARMAGNAC

Armagnac production is akin to that of Cognac, the major differences being that traditionally it is distilled only once, in a continuous still, and it is aged in local "black" oak. Armagnac's alembic consists of two containers. The first, with a "serpent" in it, is a heat exchanger, filled with cold incoming wine which is warmed by hot vapours in the serpent; the wine in turn cooling and condensing the descending distillate within the serpent. The second "container" is the still proper, heated by wood or gas. It houses a series of baffle plates and shallow reservoirs. The warmed wine from the first container coming in at the top falls onto the hot plates, overflows and gradually works its way down the still, getting hotter all the while, and vapourizing as it falls. The vapours rise to the top of the still where a crude swans neck directs them back into the first container's serpent, at the bottom of which the condensed distillate emerges at an average of 55°, considerably lower in strength than Cognac. Young Armagnac tends to be even more scented, fruity and aromatic than young Cognac because its vapours rise through falling wine, picking up primary aromas on the way.

The Cognac style pot still was outlawed in Armagnac in 1936, but permitted again from 1972 in order to make Armagnac more commercial. More "commercial" in this context meaning smoother, less earthy and fiery when young. Most Armagnacs today are therefore a blend of the two processes.

TASTING SPIRITS

"Nosing" is the best way to "taste" – if only because one's palate is rapidly numbed after tasting even a couple of spirits, especially if they are at bottle strength of around 40°. Nosing can be done as normal in a tasting glass, or one can pour a little of the spirit onto the palm of one hand, rub the palms together gently, cup them to your face and smell. This is effective because of the warmth and evaporation generated, but hardly practical for anything but a few samples. And eventually one wants to "taste" too.

1. You can "work up" a bit of saliva first, take a very small sip at bottle strength, pass it rapidly round your palate, spit almost immediately and then consider the flavour and how well it lingers.
2. More practical is to dilute the spirit with water first and then taste it as you would a wine or fortified wine. Cognac and Armagnac are best diluted to about two-thirds spirit/one-third water; Malt Whisky, being more pungent, can be diluted 50/50. It is always interesting to smell Malt Whisky neat, next to a second sample with just a **little** water added; this brings out the nose, particularly its "peet reek", in a remarkable way. This doesn't happen with any other spirit as far as I know.
3. Just for enjoyment, after a meal, try sniffing from some distance above the glass after swirling; that way the bouquet is less fierce on the nostrils; and when you sip the spirit, roll it gently round your mouth *without drawing any air through as one would with a wine,* and only open your mouth to breathe out after swallowing. The effect is similarly less fiery.

(**Above Left**) *Glasses showing the stages of Cognac distillation.* **From left to right**: *wine: 6°–8°, thin, sharp, fizzy and unclarified;* brouillis: *product of the first distillation – a sweetish smelling, watery, milky spirit of about 30°; then, from the second distillation;* heads: *a tiny proportion of harsh and literally nauseating liquid; the* heart: *which will eventually become Cognac – brilliant to behold, sweetly fruity to smell, fiery but pure and clean to taste;* seconds: *thick, dull and peppery; and* tails: *cooked, bitter, flat.*

(**Above**) *The "heart" of the second distillation, emerging from the bottom of the condensor; nascent Cognac.*

(**Opposite**) *The heart of a Cognac distillery, showing the tank which preheats the initial wine charge (**centre**); the pot still (**left**) in which wine and brouillis respectively are distilled by slow heating; the "swan's neck" (**centre left**) in which the vapourized liquids begin to condense, leading to the condenser proper (**right**) a serpentine pipe cooled in a tank of cold water at the bottom of which emerge the various distillate fractions. This is where the distiller makes his "cuts", directing the liquid into the appropriate container.*

MALT WHISKY

A beery "wash" of about 10° is to Whisky what wine is to Cognac or Armagnac. For Malt Whisky this wash is made from malted barley; barley moistened so that it will germinate, during which process its starch is converted to *maltose*, a sugar more easily assimilated by yeast and therefore more easily fermented. After germinating the barley, now called green malt, is dried in kilns, using peat for the slow, smoky fire, which imbues the malt with the "peat reek" the whiskies will eventually have. Once dried, the malt is ground and the grist mixed with local spring water to produce the sugary solution that will be fermented into the wash.

The Malt Whisky distillation process is very similar to that for Cognac. Two pot stills are used, the first to make the "low wines" (Cognac's brouillis) from the wash, the second, smaller still to produce the whisky, at a similar strength to young Cognac, in between the foreshots and feints.

Grain Whisky is made from nearly 90 per cent maize (or rice, oats, wheat etc) and a balance of barley. It is distilled by a continuous process into a highly rectified, very pure and almost flavourless spirit, emerging from the still at 94°, and immediately broken down with distilled water to 68°. It is always blended with malts and matured for a much shorter period.

(*Below*) *Peat bricks, whose slow, smoky burning dries the green malt and gives malt whisky its characteristic "peat reek"* (**left**)*.* (**Centre**) *Dried malt after grinding; this will be mixed with spring water to make the solution for distilling. And* (**right**) *uisge beatha (water of life). The first word of this gaelic phrase gave whisky its name.*

(**Right**) *Whisky stills at Bowmore in Islay. The Islay whiskies have a particularly pronounced "peat reek" and an iodine-like character (some call it medicinal, others seaweed) which distinguishes them from the mainland whiskies. Bowmore is for me the most refined of the Islays; though the most pungent and weighty, and for many the more typical expression of the island, is Laphroaig.*

PRACTICAL REFERENCE

(**Left**) *Blind tasting simply means tasting wines not knowing what they are, as they are presented in anonymous bottles. Tasting thus, without preconceptions, you assess a wine's style and quality much more objectively, relying solely on what the wine has to offer . . . and on your ability to perceive this.*

BLIND TASTING

Blind tasting wine is only "blind" in as much as you cannot see the bottle or label which identify the wine. Semi-blind tastings are those where you have some information about the wine beyond its colour; this may be a grape variety, country of origin or vintage for example. But why blind taste at all? Apart from the fun of a challenge there are more practical reasons. It forces you to rely solely on your senses and what they actually perceive, and on your own words to describe those perceptions.

DISTINGUISHING DIFFERENT STYLES

Blind tasting is the most efficient means of establish-ing what wines from different grapes and regions *really* smell and taste like *for yourself* as opposed to what you have read about them. It is one of the best ways to develop your own vocabulary, one which will mean something to you (and others with any luck) and which will help you locate, and thus perceive, more tastes and smells. You will find that many familiar words from books like this are helpful and useful, but you are bound to find other, particu-larly personal "trigger" words which will distinguish, for example, dry Riesling from Sauvignon Blanc, Cabernet Sauvignon from Syrah, or Pinot Gris from Chardonnay, just for you.

This sort of blind tasting aims at identification eventually: which grape is it and where does it come from? And it may be quite independent of any related factors such as price and winemaker's intentions.

QUALITY ASSESSMENT

Knowing what a wine is can strongly prejudice your judgement. Tasting blind will help develop your ability to assess quality, as distinct from style, because it forces you to be objective when considering quality aspects such as balance, development to the palate, harmony, length and so on; although these can never by entirely divorced from style.

If wines are compared "blind" for quality, to discover "which is best", the exercise only makes sense when similar wines are compared, or when the aim is very clear cut and specific; such as deciding which wine, of a broadly comparable type, represents best value within a given price range. Stephen Spurrier's controversial blind tastings in Paris, of Chardonnay or Cabernet-based wines from round the world, are controversial precisely because, although they have the appearance of comparing like with like (French Cabernet Sauvignon with Californian Cabernet Sauvignon; Australian Chardonnay with French Chardonnay); the differences in style between the wines are probably more significant than what they have in common, namely the grape variety. And in blind tasting where there are large numbers of wines and styles, it is the more forceful or more obviously "fruity" wines which tend to emerge as more impressive, although in more objective terms their "quality" is not necessarily better. The comparisons are interesting more for the differences in style they reveal than as a reliable guide to "which is best?" The question inevitably needs paring too: *best for what?*

BLIND TASTING IN PRACTICE

1. *Limit your aims to start with, and be clear as to what they are.* You cannot effectively taste blind for grape variety, location, vintage, quality, maturity, value for money and so on all at once.
2. *Use the wine's colour as a clue* to age and grape variety.
3. *Smell all the wines before tasting them.* Smell them when still and then after agitation. Grape variety is the most important clue to identity, and your nose the best judge of grape variety.
4. *On the palate* look for the balance of alcohol/acid/tannin as a clue to the grape and likely geographical origin; look at texture, development to the palate and length of aftertaste as a guide to quality.
5. First impressions are usually the most reliable.

6. *For purposes of identification* you need to know your grapes and geography. If you don't know what the possibilities are the odds are stacked against you!

For a more detailed examination of blind tasting for identification you cannot do better than to read Michael Broadbent's excellent section on the subject in his *Pocket Guide to Wine Tasting.*

To practise, try the following exercises, possible alone, but more practical and economical with two or more people. (You always need to hide bottle shapes, corks and capsules.) One of the best ways to memorize grape varieties and their styles is first to compare just two or three samples of the *same* type of wine or grape variety (from different producers or regions) and then compare *different* types or varieties to make the distinctions even clearer. Taste them as follows until you know them thoroughly:

1. Have a separate glass for each wine. (To avoid confusion if you are by yourself, put a small colour or number coded sticker on the underside of the glass base and corresponding wine.)
2. Taste the wines first *knowing* what they are and describe them as accurately as you can, noting any features which stand out such as dryness/sweetness, acidity, tannin, alcohol (how much or little) and any memorable characteristics on the nose.

You can then do any or all of the following progessively more difficult exercises *blind.* Wherever you fail, go back and taste the wine, knowing what it is, again to see if you can find a key feature that will help you "locate" and distinguish it.

3. Nose and taste them again *next to each other* and see if you can identify them.
4. Nose and taste them *apart,* and see if you can identify them apart.
5. Nose them *only,* next to each other . . .
6. Nose them only, *apart* . . .
7. Taste *without* nosing, next to each other . . .
8. Taste *without* nosing, *apart* . . .

In each case the aim is identification. For numbers 4–8 a friend is useful as he or she can pass you glasses in a random order and score your success or failure. If any of the wines has a very distinctive colour then nose and taste with your eyes closed.

This is an excellent way to find out how *you* identify a given style or grape variety, and also good practice at concentrating separately on different aspects of taste and smell. It is a particularly useful approach to distinguishing "confusible" varieties. The grape variety essays in Part II will suggest what to look out for.

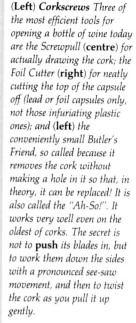

(Left) *Corkscrews Three of the most efficient tools for opening a bottle of wine today are the Screwpull (**centre**) for actually drawing the cork; the Foil Cutter (**right**) for neatly cutting the top of the capsule off (lead or foil capsules only, not those infuriating plastic ones); and (**left**) the conveniently small Butler's Friend, so called because it removes the cork without making a hole in it so that, in theory, it can be replaced! It is also called the "Ah-So!". It works very well even on the oldest of corks. The secret is not to **push** its blades in, but to work them down the sides with a pronounced see-saw movement, and then to twist the cork as you pull it up gently.*

HANDLING AND SERVING WINE

CORKSCREWS

Whatever your attachment, sentimental or otherwise, to more old fashioned corkscrews, today there is nothing to match the smooth efficiency of the Screwpull. It now has a useful partner, the Foil Cutter, which neatly removes the top of a lead capsule in a couple of seconds. If you want a slim, portable cork extractor, the two-pronged "butler's friend" or "Ah-So" is very effective, even on the oldest of corks.

DECANTING

Not to be taken too seriously! Decanting is only essential when wine has sediment in the bottle, the purpose being to separate the wine from its deposit so that what you serve is all clear and bright. Sediment mixed with the wine makes it look murky and affects the taste adversely too. It is mainly mature reds that need decanting, but it is worth examining bottles of mature white Burgundy and Bordeaux (dry and sweet) for deposit. White wine that has a fine deposit lying along the lower side of the bottle will certainly want to stand for a few hours to let this fall to the bottom, even if it doesn't seem to warrant decanting. Otherwise its brilliance will certainly be marred on pouring.

When to decant is an imponderable question. The theory is that it allows the bouquet to develop, and a firm wine to "relax" and soften. However, numerous blind tastings to test these theories have come up with inconclusive or contradictory results. Experiment allied to prejudice will eventually dictate what you do, although you will very likely find that bottle variation of the same wine plays havoc with any "controlled" experiments. As a guideline, the younger or tougher the wine the earlier in advance you can decant; the older or more delicate, the less time is required. If in doubt err on the side of too little time; bouquet is sometimes at its best early on, and if not, wines can always open up in the glass. Once they are fading or falling apart the situation is irretrievable.

Decanting can be done straight from the cellar, the bottle being kept as horizontal as possible; it is just a bit more fiddly than if you have allowed the bottle to stand and the sediment to settle for a few hours. Holding the bottle near its base, and resting the bottleneck top on the lip of the decanter makes for a steadier pouring action.

SERVING WINE: ORDER AND TEMPERATURE

Order As far as order is concerned, the same applies as for tasting, although you will probably want to be a bit more flexible. All you need to ensure is that if you have a potential clash (Sauternes and paté followed by claret with the main course for example) there is an opportunity to have a "palate cleanser" in between: water, a piece of bread or bread and butter, a morsel of hard cheese, a sorbet, a few nuts or something similar.

Temperature Of course temperature matters, but the perfect degree is a will-o-the-wisp. Quite apart from individual preference, wines taste well over a range of temperatures, albeit narrow; and what is suitable will depend not only on the style of wine but on the season, room temperature, and the temperature of any accompanying food. If you like wine, what is extreme and to be avoided will become apparent very rapidly.

Wine books usually give a thermometer indication of what is appropriate. While these may be useful, in fifteen years of wine drinking I have never used a thermometer or even thought in terms of degrees farenheit or centigrade when serving wine. The palm of my hand has been a reliable guide, winter or summer, as to whether a bottle is cold enough in the fridge or warm enough without, and my palate has usually "felt" the same. The method is certainly not unique!

White wine guidelines: cold makes drink refreshing. It gives "shape" to low acidity wines and reduces the hot and ponderous character of those that are over alcoholic. It delays the perception of acidity in tart whites and makes intense sweetness less cloying. You will generally find, the finer the wine, the less it needs to be chilled, and possibly vice versa. It is impossible to generalize about how long to leave wines in the fridge (except to say don't leave them there, they go flat) that depends on how warm they start, and how cold the fridge is. There is nothing wrong with using the freezer, you just have to remember not to forget!

Red wine guidelines How warm (or cold) you drink red wines depends mainly on how tannic (or not) they are. Warmth reduces the astringent effect of tannin, so that the more tannic a wine the warmer you will drink it, as long as it doesn't become so warm as to taste "soupy". If it is too warm the alcohol will dominate both bouquet and palate, and the wine will begin to seem hot, sharp and shapeless. *No* wine tastes good much above the comfortable room temperature of about 20°C/68°F.

Red wines with very little tannin have a structure similar to whites, with more acidity that is, and they can be "cooled", accordingly. If reds "feel" too warm, put them in the fridge for a while. With all wines, better to serve on the cool side to start with, they invariably warm up on the table.

WINE STORAGE AND CELLAR RECORDS

STORAGE

Temperature is the crucial factor; *light* and *vibration* are others. It is always easy to protect wines from light (a blanket if nothing else), and damaging extremes of vibration are going to be rare, and obvious. But wines do abhor being subjected to extremes of heat or cold, and to wide temperature variation. Cold is not usually a problem, high temperature is the bugbear. However, you can keep most wines at an average household temperature (20–21°C/68–70°F) for months without fear of damage, although they will certainly mature faster, and it is not an environment to recommend for your finer wines. At least, not for any length of time.

Young wines (not more than two to three years old) are pretty robust, and if most of your drinking is confined to these you needn't fret about cellerage. For coolness, keep them as low down as possible in the room (the temptation is to put them "up and out of the way"), where they won't need to be moved, and cover them if you can. Like ours, wines' constitutions become more delicate as they age, so mature wines, or any fine wines, should be cellared cool if they are to give of their best eventually. A fairly constant temperature between 10°–15°C (50°–60°F) is ideal.

Temperature control Perfect are an underground cellar or air conditioning; although the latter is very expensive. Temperature controlled cabinets are also available, holding from 60 to 200 bottles according to size. As big as a medium to large fridge, they are a practical, if pricey, solution for fine wine storage especially in apartments. Don't be tempted to keep the white wines too cold (below 40°) for any length of time or they will "flatten".

Insulation Whether it be cardboard boxes, blankets, polystyrene foam or whatever, can be a fickle friend. The advantage is that it does protect against *rapid* changes in ambient temperature; but it is not absolute protection. Just as it will keep cold bottles colder for longer, so it will also keep warm bottles warmer for longer once they have risen in temperature, which they will do, in permanently warm surroundings. Idle then to imagine your wines are safe insulated in the loft over a long, hot summer. They will eventually be as hot as the loft itself, and insulation will prolong the torture!

Damp cellars Bottles are kept lying on their sides to keep the corks moist and so airtight. Excess damp is not harmful to a wine's quality, although it may be a nuisance because it encourages moulds to form on bottle and label. First the labels become stained, then gradually illegible and finally they disintegrate altogether. Only a problem to lose sleep over if you have bottles of poor post war vintages of Mouton Rothschild whose labels are now worth considerably more than the wine ever was. If your labels do get very damp you need to keep a good record of what is where. Clear lacquer sprayed onto, or clingfilm wrapped around dry bottles and labels help delay the depredations of damp.

Dry cellars You would have to have an extraordinary lack of humidity to worry about corks drying and shrinking from the outside, and an excessively neurotic disposition to bother with regularly moistening gravel or sand on your cellar floor. This however is the traditional problem and its solution.

RECORDS AND CELLAR BOOKS

Once you begin to acquire more than a few dozen bottles you will find you need to keep track of just what is where, and how ready it is to drink. The more varied your bottles, the sooner this will be. A map or grid of your storage layout will avoid having to pull out numerous bottles to find the one you think you haven't drunk, and an associated cellar book will mean you can keep tabs on what you are buying, what you need to buy, what you can afford to sell – and what you have consumed! Cellar books can quickly become a fascinating record of wines you have drunk, with what and with whom; charting the development of a case, sampled over several years, a single good bottle for an occasion, or indeed one's own changing tastes. Commercial cellar books are available, but you may find it more practical to design your own page and photocopy as necessary.

(**Above**) *Various methods of supporting and separating bottles:*
Top row (bin 15): practical, free standing wood and metal racks which will accommodate bottles of any shape. These can be made to order to hold any number of bottles, half-bottles or magnums.
2nd row (bin 14): cardboard carton inners used as separators.
4th row (bin 12): provided they are supported at the side, Bordeaux bottles (parallel sided) will be stable stacked on top of each other; most other shapes are alarmingly precarious (e.g. Burgundy bottles, bin 13) and are best with wooden laths between the vertical rows.
(**Left**) *Purpose built underground cellars. In the late seventies a Frenchman named Harnois designed an underground "kit" cellar with a capacity of between 600 and 1,300 bottles according to size. These cellars provide an ideal environment, at a price similar to a small conservatory.*

WINE TO GRAPES INDEX

This index is to help you identify the grape variety(s) of a wine which you may know only by a place name.

Wines are now known by their grape variety plus place name in most countries. The most thoroughgoing exception to this is France – except for Alsace. Italy, Spain and Portugal use a mixture of place name and/or grape variety, as do the countries of Central and South Eastern Europe:

Yugoslavia, Bulgaria, Austria, Hungary, Greece and Rumania. Germany's nomenclature is based on a combination of location and grape variety (optional), whose extent and complexity put it beyond the scope of this index. The wines listed are the most commonly encountered wines made from well known grape varieties but not named after them.

LEGEND

Where one grape dominates a blend it is in **bold**.
Where a grape is not discussed in the main text of this book it is in *italics*.
Where there are additional minor grapes, not mentioned, this is shown by a + +.
Syr + Cab.S(50% max) indicates 50% maximum of any proportions of the grapes mentioned.

Abbreviations

(w)	= dry white	Alig	= Aligoté	Cins	= Cinsaut	Petit V	= Petit Verdot
(sw)	= sweet white	Cab.Fr	= Cabernet Franc	Ctx	= Côteaux	Pin Bl	= Pinot Blanc
(r)	= red	Cab.S	= Cabernet Sauvignon	Gam	= Gamay	Pin Nr	= Pinot Noir
(p)	= rosé	Cabs	= Cab.S + Cab.Fr	Gren	= Grenache	Pin Gr	= Pinot Gris
(sp)	= sparkling or pétillant	Car	= Carignan	Malb	= Malbec	Rouss	= Roussanne
VDN	= Vin Doux Naturel	Chard	= Chardonnay	Mars	= Marsanne	Sauv	= Sauvignon
Bl	= Blanc	Chen	= Chenin	Mourv	= Mourvèdre	Sem	= Semillon
B'x	= Bordeaux	Cot	is a synonym for Malbec	Nr	= Noir	Syr	= Syrah
B'y	= Burgundy						

PINOT NOIR

NAME	AREA		GRAPE(S)
Aloxe Corton	B'y	(r)	Pinot Noir
Alsace			Wines named after variety except for Edelzwicker
Anjou	Loire	(r)	**Cab.Fr**/Cab.S/*Pineau d'Aunis*
		(w)	**Chenin**(80% min)/Chardonnay/Sauvignon
		(p)	Cab.Fr/Cab.S/Gamay/*Cot*/Groslot
Anjou Ctx de La Loire		(w)	Chenin
Anjou Mousseux	Loire	(w)	**Chenin**/Cabs/*Cot*/Gamay/*Groslot*
		(p)	Cabs/*Cot*/Gamay/*Groslot*
Apremont	Savoie	(w)	**Jacquère**/Chardonnay/Aligoté
Arbois	Jura	(r)	*Poulsard*/*Trousseau*/Pinot Noir
		(w)	Savagnin/Chardonnay/Pinot Blanc
Ardèche, Ctx de L'	S Rhône	(r)	Syr/Gam/Cabs/Merl/Gren/Cins/*Car*. Some varietal wines too
		(w)	Chardonnay
Auxey Duresses	B'y	(r)	Pinot Noir
		(w)	Chardonnay
Asti Spumante	NW Italy	(sp)	Muscat
Bairrada	N Portugal	(r)	*Baga* (principal grape)
Bandol	Provence	(r)	**Mourvèdre**(50% min)/Gren/Syr/Cins
Banyuls (VDN)	Roussillon		**Grenache Noir**(50% min, 75% for Banyuls Grand Cru)/Muscats + +
Barbaresco	NW Italy	(r)	Nebbiolo
Bardolino	NE Italy	(r)	**Corvina**/*Molinara*/*Rondinella*
Barolo	NW Italy	(r)	Nebbiolo
Barsac	B'x	(sw)	**Semillon**/Sauvignon/Muscadelle
Bâtard Montrachet	B'y	(w)	Chardonnay
Béarn	SW France	(r)	**Tannat**(60% max)/Cabs/*Fer*/*Manseng* + +
Beaujolais	B'y	(r)	Gamay
		(w)	Chardonnay (Aligoté permitted)
Beaumes de Venise, Muscat de (VDN)	S Rhône		Muscat
Beaumes de Venise	S Rhône	(r)	See Côtes du Rhône Villages
Beaune	B'y	(r)	Pinot Noir
		(w)	Chardonnay
Bellet	Provence	(r)	*Braquet*/*Folle Noir*/Cinsaut + +
		(w)	*Rolle*/*Roussan* + +
Bergerac	Dordogne	(r)	Cabs/Merlot/*Malbec*
		(w, sw)	Semillon/Sauvignon/*Muscadelle*

CHARDONNAY

CABERNET FRANC

Bienvenue Bâtard-Montrachet	B'y	(w)	Chardonnay
Blagny	B'y	(r)	Pinot Noir
Blagny, Meursault-, or Puligny-Montrachet-	B'y	(w)	Chardonnay
Blanquette de Limoux	Languedoc	(sp)	**Mauzac**(70% min)/Chardonnay/Chenin
Blaye, Côtes de	Gironde	(w)	Sauvignon/Semillon/*Muscadelle* + +
Blayais		(w, sw)	Sauv/Semillon/*Muscadelle*
Blaye	Gironde		
Blaye, Premières Côtes de		(r)	Cabs/Merlot/*Malbec*
Bonnes Mares	B'y	(r)	Pinot Noir
Bonnezeaux	Loire	(sw)	Chenin Blanc
Bordeaux	Gironde	(r)	**Merlot**/Cabs/*Malbec*
		(w)	Sauvignon/Semillon/*Muscadelle*
Bourg, Côtes de Bourg, Bourgeais	B'x	(r)	Cabs/Merlot/*Malbec*
		(w)	Semillon/Sauvignon/*Muscadelle* + +
Bourgogne, Bourgogne Ordinaire,	B'y	(r)	Pinot Noir
Bourgogne Grand Ordinaire		(w)	Chardonnay/Pinot Blanc
Bourgogne Passe-tout-grains	B'y	(r)	**Gamay**/Pinot Noir(33% min)
Bourgueil, St Nicholas-de Bourgueil	Loire	(r)	**Cabernet Franc**/Cab.S(10% max)
Bouzy Rouge	Champagne	(r)	Pinot Noir/Pinot Meunier
Brouilly	Beaujolais	(r)	Gamay
Brunello di Montalcino	WC Italy	(r)	**Sangiovese**(75% min)/*Canaiolo*/*Trebbiano*/*Malvasia*
Bugey	Savoie	(r)	Gamay/Pinot Noir/*Poulsard*/*Mondeuse*
		(w)	Chard/Alig/Pin Gr/*Jacquère* + +
Buzet	SW France	(r)	**Merlot**/Cabs/*Malbec*
		(w)	Semillon/Sauvignon/*Muscadelle*
Cadillac	B'x	(sw)	Semillon/Sauvignon/*Muscadelle*
Cahors	SW France	(r)	**Auxerrois** = Malbec(70% min)/Merlot/*Tannat*
Cairanne	S Rhône	(r)	See Côtes du Rhône Villages
Canon Fronsac	B'x	(r)	Cabs/Merlot/*Malbec*
Carema	NW Italy	(r)	Nebbiolo
Carmignano	WC Italy	(r)	**Sangiovese**(45% min)/Cab.S(10% max)
Cassis	Provence	(w)	*Ugni Bl*/Sauv/*Grenache Bl*/Marsanne + +
		(r)	Grenache/Mourvèdre/Cinsaut/*Carignan*

Cérons	B'x	(sw)	**Semillon**/Sauvignon/*Muscadelle*
Chablis	B'y	(w)	Chardonnay
Chambertin		(r)	Pinot Noir
Chambertin Clos de Bèze	B'y		
Chambolle Musigny	B'y	(r)	Pinot Noir
Champagne		(sp)	Pinot Noir/Pinot Meunier/Chardonnay
Chapelle Chambertin	B'y	(r)	Pinot Noir
Charmes Chambertin	B'y	(r)	Pinot Noir
Chassagne Montrachet	B'y	(w)	Chardonnay
		(r)	Pinot Noir
Château Chalon	Jura	(w)	Savagnin
Château Grillet	N Rhône	(w)	Viognier
Chateauneuf du Pape	S Rhône	(r)	**Grenache**/Syrah/Mourvèdre/Cinsaut + +
		(w)	**Roussanne**/*Clairette*/*Bourboulenc* + +
Chenas	Beaujolais	(r)	Gamay
Chevalier Montrachet	B'y	(w)	Chardonnay
Cheverny	Loire	(w)	Chenin Bl/Chardonnay/Sauvignon
		(r)	Gamay/Cabs/Pinot Noir/*Cot*
Chianti	WC Italy	(r)	**Sangiovese**(75% min)/*Canaiolo*/*Trebbiano*/*Malvasia*
Chinon	Loire	(r)	**Cabernet Franc**/Cab.S(10% max)
Chiroubles	Beaujolais	(r)	Gamay
Chorey Lès Beaune	B'y	(r)	Pinot Noir
Clairette de Die	N Rhône	(w, sp)	*Clairette*(75% min for the dry white)/**Muscat** (50% min for the sparkling)
Clape, La	Midi		See Languedoc
Claret	B'x		English term for red Bordeaux. See: Canon-Fronsac, Fronsac, Graves, Haut-Médoc, Médoc, Margaux, Pauillac, Pomerol, St Emilion, St Estephe, St Julien (the principal appellations)
Clos de La Roche	B'y	(r)	Pinot Noir
des Lambrays	B'y	(r)	Pinot Noir
de Tart	B'y	(r)	Pinot Noir
de Vougeot	B'y	(r)	Pinot Noir
St Denis	B'y	(r)	Pinot Noir

GAMAY

Collioure	Roussillon	(r)	**Grenache**(60% min)/Syrah + Cinsaut + *Carignan*(25% min)/Mourvèdre
Condrieu	N Rhône	(w)	Viognier
Corbières	Languedoc	(r)	*Carignan*(75% max)/Cinsaut(20% max)/Syrah/Grenache/Mourvèdre
Cornas	Rhône	(r)	Syrah
Corton	B'y	(r)	Pinot Noir
Corton-Charlemagne	B'y	(w)	Chardonnay
Costières du Gard	Languedoc	(r)	*Carignan*/Grenache/Cinsaut/Syrah/Mourv
Ctx d'Aix en Provence	Provence	(r)	**Grenache**/Cins/Mourv/Syr/Cab.S/*Car*
Côteaux d'Ancennis	Loire	(r)	**Cabs**/Gamay
Côteaux du Layon	Loire	(sw)	Chenin
Côteaux du Tricastin	S Rhône		Gren/Syr/Mourv/Cins/*Car*(20% max)
Côte de Beaune			
Côte de Beaune-Village }	B'y }		see Bourgogne
Côte de Nuits-Village			
Côte Roannaise	Auvergne	(r)	Gamay
Côte Rôtie	N Rhône	(r)	**Syrah**(80% min)/Viognier
Côtes de Castillon	B'x	(r)	**Merlot**/Cab.S/Cab.F/*Malbec*
Côtes de Duras	SW France	(w)	**Sauvignon**/Sem/*Muscadelle*/Chenin/*Mauzac*
		(r)	Cabs/Merlot/*Malbec*
Côtes du Frontonnais	SW France	(r)	*Negrette*(50–70%)/Cabs/*Malb*/Syr + +
Côtes du Luberon	S Rhône	(r)	Gren/Cins/Syr/Mourv/*Car*(50% max)
Côtes du Rhône	S Rhône	(r)	**Gren**/Syr/Mourv/*Car*(30% max)
Côtes du Rhône Villages	S Rhône	(r)	**Gren**(65% max)/Syr + Mourv + Cin(25% min)/*Car*(10% max)
Côtes du Ventoux	S Rhône	(r)	As for Côtes du Rhône
Côtes du Vivarais	S Rhône	(r)	As for Côtes du Rhône
Crémant d'Alsace	Alsace	(w,sp)	Riesling/Pin Bl/Pin Nr/Pin Gr/Chard
		(p,sp)	Pinot Noir
Crémant de Bourgogne	B'y	(r, w,sp)	Pin Nr/Pin Bl/Pin Gr/Chard
Crémant de Loire		(r, w,sp)	Chen/Cab.Fr/Pin Nr/Chard + +

MERLOT

126

SYRAH

Crépy	Savoie	(w)	*Chasselas*
Coulée de Serrant	Loire	(w)	Chenin
Criots-Bâtard-Montrachet	B'y	(w)	Chardonnay
Crozes-Hermitage	N Rhône	(r)	Syrah
		(w)	**Marsanne**/Roussanne
Dôle	Switzerland	(r)	Gamay/Pinot Noir
Dorin	Switzerland	(w)	*Chasselas = Fendant*
Echézeaux	B'y	(r)	Pinot Noir
Edelzwicker	Alsace	(w)	Riesling/Gewurz/Pin Gr/Muscat/Pin Bl/Pin Nr/*Chasselas*/Sylvaner
Entre-Deux-Mers	B'x	(w)	Sauvignon/Semillon/Muscadelle
Etoile, L'	Jura	(w)	Chardonnay/*Poulsard*/Savagnin
Faugères	Languedoc	(r)	*Carignan*(50% max)/Gren + *Lladoner Pelut*(20% min)/Syr + Mourv(10% min)
Fendant	Switzerland	(w)	*Chasselas*
Fitou	Languedoc	(r)	*Carignan*(75% max)/Gren/*Lladoner Pelut* + +
Fixin	B'y	(r)	Pinot Noir
Fleurie	Beaujolais	(r)	Gamay
Frascati	WC Italy	(w)	**Malvasia**/*Trebbiano*
Franciacorta Rosso	NW Italy	(r)	**Cabs**/Barbera/Nebbiolo/Merlot
Fronsac	B'x	(r)	Merlot/Cab.Fr/Cab.S/*Malbec*
Frontignan, Muscat de (VDN)	Languedoc		Muscat
Gaillac	SW France	(w, sp)	*Len de L'El*/*Mauzac*/Sem/Sauv + +
		(r, p)	*Duras* + Fer + Gam + Syr(60% min)/Cabs/Merlot
Gard, Costières du	Languedoc	(r)	*Car*(50% max)/Gren(25% min from 1990)/Mourv + Syr(15% min by 1995)
Gavi	NW Italy	(w)	*Cortese*
Gattinara	NW Italy	(r)	Nebbiolo
German wines			See text entries: Riesling, Müller Thurgau, Sylvaner, Gewürztraminer, Scheurebe, Kerner, Pinot Noir
Gevrey Chambertin	B'y	(r)	Pinot Noir
Gevrey Chambertin Clos St Jacques	B'y	(r)	Pinot Noir

GRENACHE / GARNACHA

Ghemme	NW Italy	(r)	Nebbiolo
Gigondas	S Rhône	(r)	**Grenache**(80% max)/Syr + Mourv(15% min)/Cinsaut(10% max)
Givry	B'y	(r)	Pinot Noir
		(w)	Chardonnay
Grands Echezeaux	B'y	(r)	Pinot Noir
Graves	B'x	(r)	Cab.S/Merl/Cab.Fr/*Malbec*/*Petit V*
		(w)	Semillon/Sauvignon/*Muscadelle*
Graves de Vayres	B'x	(r)	As for Graves
Griottes-Chambertin	B'y	(r)	Pinot Noir
Haut Médoc	B'x	(r)	**Cab.S**/Merl/Cab.Fr/*Malbec*/*Petit V*
Haut Poitou	Loire	(r)	**Gamay**/Pin Nr/Merlot/Cabs
		(w)	**Sauvignon**/Chard/Pin Bl/Chenin
Hermitage	N Rhône	(r)	**Syrah**/Mars + Rouss(15% max)
		(w)	Roussanne/Marsanne
Irancy, Bourgogne-	B'y	(r)	**Pinot Noir**/*César*/*Tressot*
Irouleguy	SW France	(r)	Cabs(50% min)/*Tannat*
		(w)	*Courbu*/*Manseng*
Jasnières	Loire	(w)	Chenin
Juliénas	Beaujolais	(r)	Gamay
Jura (Côtes du-)	EC France	(r)	Pin Nr/Pin Gr/*Poulsard*/*Trousseau*
		(w)	Chardonnay/Savagnin
Jurançon	SW France	(w, sw)	*Manseng*(Petit and Gros)/*Courbu* + +
Ladoix	B'y	(r)	See Bourgogne
Lalande-de-Pomerol	B'x	(r)	**Merlot**/Cabs/*Malbec*
Languedoc, Ctx du	Midi	(r)	*Carignan*(50% max)/Cinsaut(50% max)/Mourv and/or Syr(10% min from 1990)/Gren and/or *Lladoner Pelut*(20% min from 1990, if *Carignan* used in blend) + +
La Clape, Languedoc		(r)	See Languedoc
		(w)	***Bourboulenc***(60% min from 1990)/*Clairette*/*Grenache Blanc* + +

Latricières-Chambertin	B'y	(r)	Pinot Noir
Lavilledieu	SW France	(r)	**Negrette**(35% min)/*Mauzac* + +
Lessona	NW Italy	(r)	Nebbiolo
Lirac	S Rhône	(r, p)	**Grenache**(40% min)/*Car*(10% max)/Syr/Cins/Mourv
Listrac	B'x	(r)	**Cab.S**/Merlot/Cab.Fr/*Malbec*/*Petit V*
Loupiac	B'x	(sw)	**Semillon**/Sauvignon/*Muscadelle*
Luberon (Côtes du-)	S Rhône	(r)	*Carignan*(50% max)/Gren/Syr/Cins/Mourv
		(w)	*Clairette*/*Bourboulenc* + +
Lussac-St-Emilion	B'x	(r)	**Merlot**/Cab.Fr/Cab.S/*Malbec*
Lyonnais (Ctx du-)	Beaujolais	(r)	Gamay
		(w)	Chardonnay/Aligoté
Mâcon	B'y	(r)	Gamay/Pin Nr/Pin Gr
		(w)	Chardonnay/Pin Bl
Madiran	SW France	(r)	**Tannat**(40% min, 60% max)/Cabs/*Fer*
Margaux	B'x	(r)	**Cab.S**/Merlot/Cab.Fr/Malbec/Petit V
Marmandais	SW France	(r)	Cabs + Merlot(75% max)/*Cot*/*Fer*/Gamay/Syr + +
Marsannay	B'y	(r)	Pinot Noir
Maury (VDN)	Midi		Grenache(50% min)/Muscats + +
Mazis-Chambertin	B'y	(r)	Pinot Noir
Médoc	B'x	(r)	See Haut-Médoc
Menetou Salon	Loire	(w)	Sauvignon
		(r)	Pinot Noir
Mercurey	B'y	(r)	Pinot Noir
		(w)	Chardonnay
Meursault	B'y	(w)	Chardonnay
		(r)	Pinot Noir
Minervois	SW France	(r)	**Carignan**(60% max from 1990)/Gren + +
			(Syr + Cins + Mourv + *Lladonner*: 30% min, as a group, from 1990 + +)
Monbazillac	B'x	(sw)	**Semillon**/Sauvignon/*Muscadelle*

NEBBIOLO

129

Montagny	B'y	(w)	Chardonnay
Monthélie	B'y	(r)	Pinot Noir
Montlouis	Loire	(w, sp)	Chenin
Montrachet	B'y	(w)	Chardonnay
Montravel	Dordogne	(w)	**Sauvignon**/Semillon/*Muscadelle* + +
Morellino di Scansano	WC Italy	(r)	**Sangiovese**/other black grapes (15% max)
Morey St Denis	B'y	(r)	Pinot Noir
Morgon	Beaujolais	(r)	Gamay
Moulin à Vent	Beaujolais	(r)	Gamay
Moulis	B'x	(r)	**Cab.S**/Merlot/Cab.Fr/*Malbec/Petit V*
Musar (Château)	Lebanon	(r)	**Cab.S**/Syrah/Cinsaut
Muscadet	Loire	(w)	Muscadet (= Melon de Bourgogne)
Musigny	B'y	(r)	Pinot Noir
Nuits St George	B'y	(r)	Pinot Noir
Orléanais, Vins de l'	Loire	(r)	Pin Nr/Pinot Meunier/Cabs
Orvieto	WC Italy	(w)	*Trebbiano* (50% min) + +
Pacherenc du Vic Bilh	SW France	(w, sw)	*Manseng*(Petit and Gros)/*Raffiat de Moncade/Courbu*/Sauvignon/Semillon
Pauillac	B'x	(r)	**Cab.S**/Merlot/Cab.Fr/*Malbec/Petit V*
Pécharmant	Dordogne	(r)	Cabs/Merlot/Malbec
Pernand-Vergelesses	B'y	(r)	Pinot Noir
		(w)	Chardonnay
Pierrevert, Ctx du	S Rhône	(r)	*Carignan*/Cins/Gren/Mourv/Syr + +
		(w)	*Clairette*/Mars/Rouss/*Ugni Bl*
Pomerol	B'x	(r)	**Merlot**/Cab.Fr/Cab.S
Pommard	B'y	(r)	Pinot Noir
Pouilly-Fuissé	B'y	(w)	Chardonnay
Pouilly-Fumé	Loire	(w)	Sauvignon
Pouilly-Loché	B'y	(w)	Chardonnay
Pouilly-Vinzelles	B'y	(w)	Chardonnay

SAUVIGNON BLANC

SEMILLON

Pouilly sur Loire	Loire	(w)	**Chasselas** with or without Sauvignon
Provence, Côtes de	Provence	(r, p)	*Carignan*(40% max)/Syrah/Cab.S/Mourv/Cins/Gren + +
		(w)	*Clairette*/Semillon/*Ugni Blanc* + +
Puligny-Montrachet	B'y	(w)	Chardonnay
Quarts de Chaume	Loire	(sw)	Chenin
Quincy	Loire	(w)	Sauvignon
Rasteau (VDN)	S Rhône		**Grenache** (90% min)
Rasteau	S Rhône	(r)	See Côtes du Rhône
Reuilly	Loire	(w)	Sauvignon
		(r, p)	Pinot Noir/Pinot Gris
Riceys, Rosé de	Champagne	(p)	Pinot Noir
Richebourg	B'y	(r)	Pinot Noir
Rioja	N Spain	(r)	**Tempranillo**/Garnacho/*Graziano*/*Mazuelo* + +
		(w)	*Malvasia*/*Viura*
Rivesaltes (VDN)	S Rhône		Grenache/Muscats/*Maccabéo* + +
Rivesaltes, Muscat de (VDN)	S Rhône		Muscats
Roches aux Moines	Loire	(w)	Chenin
Roero	NW Italy	(r)	Nebbiolo
Romanée, La	B'y	(r)	Pinot Noir
Romanée-Conti	B'y	(r)	Pinot Noir
Romanée-St-Vivant	B'y	(r)	Pinot Noir
Rosé d'Anjou	Loire	(p)	Cabs/*Pineau d'Aunis*/Gamay/*Cot*/*Groslot*
Rosso Conero	EC Italy	(r)	**Montepulciano**/Sangiovese
Roussillon (Côtes du)		(r, p, w)	**Carignan** (70% max)/Syr + Mourv (10% min)/gren/*cins*/*Lladoner*
			Pelut/*Maccabéo*
Ruchottes-Chambertin	B'y	(r)	Pinot Noir
Rully	B'y	(r)	Pinot Noir
		(w)	Chardonnay
St Amour	Beaujolais	(r)	Gamay
St Aubin	B'y	(r)	Pinot Noir
		(w)	Chardonnay
St Chinian	Midi	(r)	*Carignan*(50% max)/Gren + *Lladoner Pelut*(20% min)/Syr + Mourv(10% min)
St Croix du Mont	B'x	(sw)	**Semillon**/Sauvignon/*Muscadelle*

ALIGOTÉ

St Emilion	B'x	(r)	**Merlot**/Cabs/*Malbec*
St Estephe	B'x	(r)	**Cab.S**/Merlot/Cab.Fr/*Malbec/Petit V*
St Joseph	N Rhône	(r)	Syrah
		(w)	Marsanne/Roussanne
St Julien	B'x	(r)	**Cab.S**/Merlot/Cab.Fr/*Malbec/Petit V*
St Nicholas de Bourgeuil	Loire		See Bourgeuil
St Peray	Rhône	(w, sp)	Marsanne/Roussanne
St Pourçain	Auvergne	(r)	**Gamay**/Pinot Noir
		(w)	*Tressalier*(50% max)/Chard/Sauv/Alig/*St Pierre Doré*(10% max)
St Romain	B'y	(r)	Pinot Noir
		(w)	Chardonnay
St Véran	B'y	(w)	Chardonnay
Sancerre	Loire	(w)	Sauvignon
		(r)	Pinot Noir
Santenay	B'y	(r)	Pinot Noir
Saumur	Loire	(w)	**Chenin**(80% min)/Chard + Sauv(20% max)
		(r)	Cabs/*Pineau d'Aunis*
Saumur Champigny	Loire	(r)	Cabs/*Pineau d'Aunis*
Saumur Mousseux	Loire	(sp: w, p)	**Chenin**/Chard + Sauv(20% max)/Cabs/Gamay/Pin Nr/*Groslot/Pineau d'Aunis*(60% max of red grapes)
Sauternes	B'x	(sw)	**Semillon**/Sauvignon/*Muscadelle*
Savennières	Loire	(w)	Chenin
Savigny-Lès-Beaune	B'y	(r)	Pinot Noir
		(w)	Chardonnay
Savoie, Vin de	EC France	(w, sp)	*Jacquère*/Chard/Aligoté/*Altesse* + +
		(r, p)	Gamay/*Mondeuse*/Pinot Noir + +
Seyssel	EC France	(w)	*Roussette*
Seyssel Mousseux	France	(sp)	*Roussette*(10% min)/*Chasselas/Molette*
Soave	NE Italy	(w)	***Garganega***/*Trebbiano*
Spanna	NW Italy	(r)	Nebbiolo
Tâche, La	B'y	(r)	Pinot Noir
Taurasi	EC Italy	(r)	*Aglianico*

Tavel	S Rhône	(p, r)	**Gren**/Cins(15% min)/*Car*(10% max)/Syr/Mourv + +
Thoursais, Vins de	Loire	(w)	Chenin(80% min)/Chard
		(r, p)	Cabs/Gamay
Tokay d'Alsace	Alsace	(w)	Pinot Gris
Tokay (Tokaji)	Hungary	(w, sw)	Furmint/Harslevelü
Torgiano	WC Italy	(r)	Sangiovese(50% min)/*Canaiolo*/*Trebbiano*
Toul, Côtes de	NE France	(r)	Pinot Meunier/Pinot Noir
		(p)	Gamay/Pinot Meunier/Pinot Noir
		(w)	Aligoté/*Auxerrois Blanc*
Touraine	Loire	(w)	Chenin/Sauv/*Arbois*/Chard(20% max)
		(r)	Cabs/*Cot*/Gamay/Pin Nr/Pin Gr + +
		(p)	Cabs/*Cot*/Gamay/Pin Nr/Pin Gr/*Groslot* + +
Tricastin, Ctx du	S Rhône	(r, p)	Gren/Syr/Cins/Mourv/*Car*(20% max)
		(w)	*Clairette*/*Gren Bl*/*Bourboulenc*/*Ugni Bl*(30% max)/*Picpoul Bl*
Tursan	SW France	(r)	**Tannat**(75% max)/Cabs + *Fer*(25% min)
		(w)	**Barroque**(90% min)/Sauv/Manseng + +
Vacqueyras	S Rhône	(r)	See Côtes du Rhône Villages
Valençay	Loire	(r, p)	Cabs/*Cot*/Pin Nr/Gamay + +
		(w)	Chard + Sauv + *Arbois*(60% min)/Chenin + +
Valpolicella	NE Italy	(r)	**Corvina**/*Molinara*/*Rondinella*
Valtellina	NW Italy	(r)	Nebbiolo
Vega Sicilia	NW Spain	(r)	Cab.S/Merlot/Malbec + +
Ventoux, Côtes du	S Rhône	(r)	Gren/Syr/Cins/Mourv/*Car*(30% max)
		(w)	**Clairette**/**Bourboulenc** + +
Vinho Verde	N Portugal	(w)	*Alvarhino*/*Loureiro*
Vin Jaune	Jura	(w)	Savagnin
Vin Nobile de Montipulciano	WC Italy	(r)	**Sangiovese**(75% min)/*Canaiolo*/*Trebbiano*/*Malvasia*
Vivarais, Côtes du	S Rhône	(r)	Gren/Syr/Mourv/Cins/*Car*(30% max)
Volnay	B'y	(r)	Pinot Noir
Vosne Romanée	B'y	(r)	Pinot Noir
Vougeot	B'y	(r)	Pinot Noir
Vouvray	Loire	(w, sw)	Chenin

SANGIOVESE

GLOSSARY

AC Appellation Contrôlée: official French designation which guarantees the area from which a wine has come, the method by which and grapes with which, it has been made.
Acescent The specific nail varnish-like smell of ETHYL ACETATE, a by-product of the formation of ACETIC acid. An acescent wine is faulty. (See VOLATILE ACIDITY.)
Acetaldehyde Produced by the oxidation of alcohol. Naturally present in imperceptible quantities in light white wines. Has a heavy, sweetish smell normal in deliberately oxidized, fortified wines like sherry; but such a smell in light white wines indicates excess oxydation. (See MADERIZED.)
Acetic Smelling and tasting of acetic acid, i.e. vinegar. (See VOLATILE, VOLATILE ACIDITY.)
Acid/Acidity 1. Essential component of wine which preserves it, enlivens and shapes its flavours and helps prolong its aftertaste.
2. Acid, as a tasting term on its own, describes an unacceptably high level of acidity.
Acrid A pungent, piquant and sometimes burning sensation due to excess SULPHUR. Felt at the top of the nostrils and back of the throat. (See SULPHUR DIOXIDE.)
Aftertaste The sensations of taste (and smell) which persist after one has swallowed or spat a wine. (See LENGTH.)
Aggressive Unpleasantly harsh in taste or texture, usually due to a high level of TANNIN or ACID.
Alcoholic Describes wines with too much alcohol and which taste uncharacteristically "heavy" or "hot" as a result.
Almacenista Specialist stockist of fine sherries.
Anthocyanins Substances in the skin of black grapes which produce the vivid purple colour in young wines.
Aroma Technically the smells coming from the grape itself as opposed to those from vinification and/or ageing in barrel or bottle. Loosely interchangeable with BOUQUET.
Aromatic Applied to wines from grape varieties with a pronounced and distinctive aroma (e.g. Sauvignon Blanc, Cabernet Sauvignon) usually with a SPICY, slightly pungent quality. Also describes that part of the flavour or aftertaste which is smelled rather than tasted.
Astringent Drying, puckering effect on the gums produced by TANNIN modifying the lubricant properties of saliva. A high level of ACIDITY can produce a similar effect.
Austere A hard, unyielding feel due to ACIDITY and/or TANNIN, usually said of young wines which need time to soften.
Backward Less developed and mature than expected for its age or type.
Balance The relationship between alcohol, ACID, TANNIN and flavour in a wine, that varies according to the wine's style and its origin. (See WELL BALANCED.)
Barrique Small oak barrels (225 litres in Bordeaux) in which wine is aged for a period before being bottled.
Bite A marked degree of ACIDITY – usually complimentary.
Blackcurrant The smell commonly associated with Cabernet Sauvignon. Needs qualifying: raw blackcurrants, cooked blackcurrants, blackcurrant jam, cassis, etc.
Blowsy Wines that are *high* in alcohol and flavour, but that are also shapeless and SHORT because they *lack* ACIDITY (many 1983 white Burgundies).
Blunt Strong in flavour and often ALCOHOLIC, but lacking in AROMATIC interest and DEVELOPMENT ON THE PALATE (many 1975 Clarets).
Body The impression of weight and consistency in the mouth due to a combination of alcohol and concentration of flavour. A complex concept, not solely due to alcohol.
Botrytis See NOBLE ROT.
Bouquet Technically refers to smells resulting from vinification and/or barrel and bottle ageing as opposed to the smells due to the grape itself. Loosely interchangeable with AROMA.
Breed Used of wines with particularly REFINED qualities.
Brut Either "dry", as in Champagnes, or "unfinished" wine – a sample drawn from the vat, for example, is known as *vin brut*.
Buttery The smell of melted butter, usually associated with rich Chardonnay wines. Used to describe colour as well.
Caramel The smell and/or taste of caramelized sugar – often with a slightly burnt character.
Carbon dioxide/CO_2 Carbonic gas. Along with ethyl alcohol the principal product of alcoholic fermentation.
Carbonic maceration Fermentation using whole bunches of intact grapes in a CO_2 saturated atmosphere. Makes fruity, well coloured wines with barely any tannin for drinking early. Initially associated with Beaujolais.
Casky The unpleasant smell of damp and rotting wood from old or unclean casks. A fault.
Cedary/Cedar wood The smell of cedar wood associated with mature Claret and Cabernet Sauvignon aged in new French oak; occasionally found in oak aged white wines too.
Chalky An impression of "chalkiness" from the soil that is associated with many wines from the Loire – Cabernet Franc especially. Similar to EARTHY.
Chaptalization The addition of sugar to the MUST early on during fermentation in order to increase a wine's alcohol content. Often misunderstood. *All* the sugar is converted to alcohol and the process is not used to "sweeten".
Cigar box Another description for CEDAR WOOD.
Citrus fruit The smells and flavours associated with citrus fruits, often found in wines where citric acid has been added – lemon, lime and grapefruit characteristics in particular.
Claret Red wine from Bordeaux.
Classed growth *Cru Classé* in French. Refers to the 1855 classification of Bordeaux Châteaux in the Médoc which ranked the top 60 or so properties into five *Crus* (1st Growth to 5th Growth) on the basis of prices achieved up to that time. The classification is quite independent of the Bordeaux AC's.
Clean Free of faults. Does not necessarily imply good quality.
Clone Clonal selection reproduces vine stock from cuttings of a single vine with particularly desirable virtues.
Closed Implies that there are qualities in the wine but that they are not yet "showing".
Cloying Sweetness which appears excessive or "sticky" because there is inadequate ACIDITY to balance it.
Coarse Usually refers to texture, particularly that due to TANNIN, but also used to describe large, harsh bubbles in sparkling wines.
Common A more damning way of saying ordinary.
Complete For a given level, not lacking in any aspect of BOUQUET, PALATE and AFTERTASTE.
Complex Multiplicity of flavours and nuance, both in taste and smell. A hallmark of quality.
Constitution A wine's basic physical make up – of alcohol, acid, fruit concentration and (for red wines) tannin – as distinct from its actual tastes or quality. Structure means the same thing.
Corked/corky A mouldy, dusty smell in the wine due to a mould affected cork.
Creamy 1. The rich, smooth *texture* of Champagne with a fine mousse giving a cream-like impression on the palate.
2. The *smell* of young, rich Merlot, usually from Pomerol, and marked by new oak. A combination of associations – the texture and smell of fresh cream, the aroma of "vanilla-pod" sugar.
Crémant Champagne with softer, gentler mousse than normal.
Crisp A lively, attractive ACIDITY in a white wine – the kind you want in a juicy apple.
Crust The substantial deposit formed in bottles of mature vintage port.
Dégorgement Removal of the sediment produced by the second fermentation in a Champagne bottle. (English disgorgement.)
Delicate Light but REFINED wine.
Dense Concentration of aromas on the nose, an almost palpable abundance.
Depth Mouthfilling layers of flavour, usually accompanied by a long DEVELOPMENT ON THE PALATE.
Developed/undeveloped Refers to a wine's readiness to drink.
Development on/to the palate A quality criterion referring to taste and texture sensations, and how they are sustained, vary and evolve during the time the wine is kept on the palate.
Distinctive Marked individuality of style.
Distinguished Exceptional character and quality.
DO Spanish version of AC.
DOC/DOCG Italian version of AC.
Drive A word of Hugh Johnson's, I believe. An evocative adjective to describe a vigorous development to the palate.
Drying out Losing fruit (or sweetness in sweet wines) to the extent that acid, alcohol or tannin dominate the taste. At this stage the wine will not improve.
Dull Simply, dull!
Dumb Another word for CLOSED usually referring to bouquet . . . little now, greatness to come.
Earthy The impression on the nose (and as an aroma on the palate) of damp earth, usually used in a positive sense.
Eiswein Wine made from grapes picked and pressed while frozen. Because a proportion of water in the juice remains as ice, it is not expressed during pressing and the must is therefore particularly concentrated in sugar.
Elegant REFINED flavours, HARMONIOUS balance, and absence of any harshness.
Elevage The care and treatment of wine in vat or barrel prior to bottling.
Empty Similar to HOLLOW – empty of flavour and interest.
Encepagement The mix of different grape varieties in a vineyard or wine, from the French *cépage* meaning grape variety.
Estufagem The heating process undergone by Madeira, from the Portuguese *estufa* meaning an oven.
Ethyl acetate A substance which smells like nail varnish or very strong pear drops and known as the fault of ACESCENCE when it can be clearly smelled in a wine. Usually associated with, though quite distinct from, VOLATILE ACIDITY. (See OXIDIZED.)
Eucalyptus A smell associated with many Australian red wines.
Farmyardy Animal and vegetable smells, usually found in mature Merlot or Pinot Noir.
Fierce Wines that are harsh and aggressive from a combination of high alcohol *and* high acidity.
Filter pads Overused filter pads often leave a smell of wet paper or cardboard. Pour a wine through coffee filter papers and smell it afterwards; the impression is the same.
Filtration Filtration removes larger particles than FINING by a physical sieving process. It is a coarser clarifying process than fining.
Fine A general term for a wine of good quality. Not the same as REFINED.
Fining Removal of particles in a wine that are too small to be filtered out. They are removed by electrochemical separation using a fining agent such as egg white.
Finish Sensations of taste and texture experienced as and after you swallow or spit a wine. (See AFTERTASTE, LENGTH.)
Firm A noticeable acidity but not excessive – a positive quality, especially in young wines which need time to mature.
Fixed acidity Refers to the non VOLATILE wine acids, tartaric and malic acid being the most important.
Flabby Seriously lacking in ACIDITY.
Flat Lacking in BOUQUET, fresh flavours and ACIDITY. Of a sparkling wine, one that has lost its bubble.
Fleshy Mainly for red wines – rich in flavour, a palpable consistency. Soft and smooth in texture with very little tannin.
Flinty Another earthy/minerally impression usually associated with crisp, dry white wines such as Sancerre or Chablis.
Flor Surface yeast which forms on Fino Sherry and Vin Jaune in barrel.
Floral/flowery Scent and aroma reminiscent of flowers both on nose and palate – German Rieslings especially.
Forward Mature and ready to drink earlier than expected for age and style.
Fragrant A delicate, perfumed, scented character on the nose.
Free run wine Red wine run off the skins from the fermenting vat leaving behind the saturated mass of skins from which the PRESS WINE is obtained.
Fresh Youthful and lively, referring particularly to an appealing ACIDITY.
Fruity Overworked but difficult to avoid. Always indicates lots of fruit flavour, and often implies not much else!
Full In BODY and/or flavour.
Glassy A word I use to describe a particularly smooth but rather unyielding texture, like glass, found mainly in fine Riesling, Semillon and Chenin wines.
Glossy The exceptionally smooth and polished feel of very fine mature wine with all its youthful edges gone.
Glycerol An alcohol produced during fermentation contributing to the sweetness of a wine, rarely to its texture.
Gooseberry For many, the best description of young and aromatic Sauvignon Blanc.
Governo Tuscan process of adding a small proportion of semi-dried grapes or concentrated must to fermented wine to induce a slight refermentation, and to increase freshness and bouquet.
Graceful Wines that are not forceful, but harmonious and pleasing in a quiet way.
Grand Cru Top rank vineyard and wine in Burgundy. The Grand Cru designation is part of the AC hierarchy in Burgundy. (See CLASSED GROWTH.)
Grapefruit The aroma one often finds in wines acidified with citric acid, and possibly also a consequence of fermenting with certain selected yeast strains. The grapefruity smell of many Australian white wines may well be due to either or both of these.

Grapey A strong impression of the grape in its raw form – exemplified by sweet Muscats such as Beaumes de Venise.
Gravelly The specific earthyness associated with Médoc wines, from Pauillac, St. Julien and Graves in particular. However absurd it seems, it is difficult to ignore once suggested.
Green As with unripe fruit, too high in acidity and lacking RIPE flavour.
Grip A welcome firmness (but not coarseness) of texture, usually from TANNIN, which helps give definition to wines such as Claret and Port.
Halbtrocken German wines with a maximum of 18g/l of residual sugar. Literally, half-dry.
Hard Pronounced firmness of texture due to TANNIN and/or ACIDITY. Usually in young wines needing time to mellow.
Harmonious Well balanced proportions with no constituent being either obtrusive or lacking, and *all* the individual "parts" mellowed and married. (Immature wines can be WELL BALANCED but not yet harmonious.)
Harsh In texture.
Heavy High in alcohol, objectively. Usually used in a critical sense, implying inadequate balancing acidity.
Hollow Lacking in flavour and very SHORT.
Hot Excessive alcohol producing a warm-to-burning sensation, especially on the FINISH.
Hydrogen sulphide/H_2S Smell of bad eggs or rubber (See MERCAPTANS, REDUCED.)
Inky A word I use only for an impenetrable depth of colour. Others use it to convey an unpleasant metallic/tinny flavour.
Jug-wine A nicer way of saying "plonk".
Lactic acid (See MALOLACTIC FERMENTATION.)
Lanolin A rich, waxy impression, occasionally recalling polish, which is found on mature Sauternes, or Semillon based wines.
Lean Not necessarily critical, but describing a rather austere style. As a term of criticism: lacking in fruit, and possibly astringent too.
Lees The sediment deposited by young wines in barrel or vat, consisting mainly of inactive yeasts and small particles of solid matter from the grape. (*Lie* in French.)
Lemony Self explanatory – useful for dry white wine description.
Length/long The length of time for which the sensations of taste and AROMA persist after swallowing. The longer the better.
Light In body and/or flavour.
Lively Of acidity, giving an attractive zip and definition to a wine. Complimentary.
Loose knit Not quite flabby, but implies a lack of acidity, poorly defined flavours.
Lustrous A noticeable quality in the appearance of the very finest wines.
Maceration The steeping of the grape's solid matter in the MUST and/or wine where alcohol acts as a solvent to extract colour, tannin and aroma from the skins.
Maderized A critical term for OXIDIZED white wine that has darkened in colour and become flat, then stale. The stage *before* VOLATILE and/or ACESCENT.
Malic acid The "green" appley acid that the grape feeds on as it matures.
Malolactic fermentation The process by which bacteria (as opposed to yeast) change MALIC ACID to softer lactic acid.
Matt The texture of young red wine with a fine quality tannin which is still matt in feel rather than GLOSSY.
Mature Ready to drink.
Mean High in acid, low in flavour – charmless wine.
Meaty Not a word I use, but for others it means wines (usually red) with plenty of matter and a "chewy" quality.
Mellow Soft and without harshness; but well balanced, not flabby.
Mercaptans Foul substances smelling of garlic, sweat and worse; the consequence of severe REDUCTION.
Minerally Aromas on nose and palate that I find on wines from volcanic and granite soils (N. Rhône, Oregon, Tokay, etc).
Mint A smell often found on Californian Cabernets. Not far from Eucalyptus which, for me, is an Australian characteristic.
Mistelle Unfermented grape juice fortified with grape spirit to prevent fermentation.
Musk The heady, heavy scent that is part of the smell of BOTRYTIS and/or mature Semillon – the two are not unconnected!
Must Juice from grapes before it has been fermented into wine.
Neutral Pleasant but without any distinctive characteristics.
Noble rot *Botrytis Cinerea* – grey rot which, under certain conditions, affects and transforms white grapes which then make remarkable sweet white wine. In these cases the rot is "noble".
Nouveau Wine made to be drunk very young, *primeur* means the same thing.
Nutty The smell of various nuts (rarely specified) usually associated with mature Chardonnay from Burgundy; also found on fine amontillado sherries.
Oaky The VANILLARY, CEDARY or TOASTY smell and dry texture that comes from ageing wines in casks made from new oak (cf woody).
Oily Can refer to texture, where it is uncomplimentary; or to the BOUQUET of mature Riesling or Semillon, where it is a very desirable quality.
Old Not just an objective description of age, but a pejorative term for wine that is past its best; tired, fading or DRYING OUT.
Oxydized In general refers to the series of faults resulting from excess contact with oxygen. More specifically, the flat, bitter-sweet or caramelly stage in red wines before they become VOLATILE or ACESCENT. (See also MADERIZED.)
Palate "On the palate" is "in the mouth".
Papery (See FILTER PADS.)
Peak The period of time during which a wine tastes at its best. Very subjective.
Penetrating Of BOUQUET: very concentrated and clear cut, a quality aspect.
Peppery A distinct impression of pepperiness (ground black pepper) found in many Rhône wines and in Ports.
Perfumed (See FRAGRANT.)
Pétillant Lightly sparkling.
Petrolly An attractive smell, reminiscent of oils, petrol, paraffin in the most agreeable way, that is found on mature Riesling especially, and to a lesser extent on mature Semillon.
Potent Alcoholic, therefore forceful.
Premier Cru Second rank (AC) in Burgundy. First rank (1855 Classification) in Bordeaux. (See CLASSED GROWTH and GRAND CRU.)
Press wine Red wine "pressed" from the saturated mass of skins after the FREE RUN wine has been drained from the fermenting vat. Kept separately and/or used for blending.
Pricked A vivid description for a wine smelling of ACETIC acid.
Prickle The delicate sensation of carbon dioxide on the tip of the tongue from a "still" wine – in contrast to the mousse of a sparkling wine.
Racking Periodic decanting of bright wine from one barrel to another in order to separate it from LEES; to eliminate carbon dioxide; or to give it a limited contact with oxygen.
Racy A combination of finesse and exciting DEVELOPMENT TO THE PALATE; a noticeably thoroughbred feel.
Rancio A Spanish word used to describe the pleasant buttery/nutty smells of acetals. These are formed by the slow combination of aldehydes (such as ACETALDEHYDE) and alcohol. The term is associated mainly with fine old sherries, Banyuls and cognacs that have spent many years in cask.
Raw Young wine whose elements of alcohol, ACIDITY and TANNIN, not yet mellowed and married, make for harsh, raw impressions.
Reduced/Reduction Indicates smells resulting from sulphur combined with hydrogen as opposed to oxygen. (See HYDROGEN SULPHIDE, cf SULPHUR DIOXIDE.)
Refined A total absence of coarseness in flavour and texture.
Residual sugar Sugar that remains in the finished wine because it has not been fermented.
Rich Abundance of flavour, opulence of texture. Does not mean sweet. The current fashion for describing Sauternes as "rich" to indicate sweet rather than dry white Bordeaux is plain silly!
Ripe Natural sweetness of flavour resulting from fully ripe grapes, not from RESIDUAL SUGAR.
Robust Full-bodied, vigorous wine but with an unrefined, maybe rough texture.
Rotten eggs The most common smell associated with HYDROGEN SULPHIDE (H_2S).
Rubbery Another smell associated with HYDROGEN SULPHIDE.
Rustic A term, usually critical, to describe wine made by the worst of old-fashioned methods and therefore usually coarse.
Savoury Particularly tasty with a suggestion of spices.
Sharp Acidity verging on being unpleasant.
Short In AFTERTASTE. Quality wines are "long".
Silky A particularly smooth, enveloping texture found, for example, in mature Sauternes and red Burgundy.
Smoky An aromatic character in some Sauvignon Blancs from the Loire especially; I also find smoky qualities in some Syrah wines from the N. Rhône, and in fine Bual and Sercial Madeiras.
Soft Usually complimentary but may need qualifying. Refers to the texture of TANNIN and/or level of ACIDITY in particular.
Spicy Self-explanatory – often a quality of fine Pomerols, also of Gewürztraminer.
Stalky/stemmy Coarse, "green" astringency derived from unripe grapes, excessive pressing or excessive maceration. Mainly red, occasionally white wines.
Steely A severe ACIDITY in good quality white wine. Eg: young Alsace Riesling.
Stewed Strong red wines with little aromatic character and low acidity, usually from hot climatic conditions, fermentation at too high a temperature, or excess MACERATION. The analogy is with stewed tea, infused for too long.
Structure See CONSTITUTION
Subtle A complexity and refinement which are not obvious.
Sulphur An antiseptic commonly used in winemaking. Used with care it is harmless and undetectable. Used in excess it creates unpleasant faults.
Sulphur Dioxide/SO_2 Excess SO_2 has a pungent, pricking smell when sniffed sharply and it causes an acrid, catching sensation in the throat.
Supple Softness of texture; in red wines the texture of good quality TANNIN from ripe grapes and careful winemaking.
Sweet Mainly used for white, dessert and fortified wines, and indicates sweetness from residual sugar. (See RIPE.)
Tannin A substance found in the skins and pips of grapes. Preserves wine and accounts for the ASTRINGENT "puckering" effect in red wines.
Tart Sharp, green, excess ACIDITY.
Tartaric acid The principal acid in wine.
Tartrate crystals White (or purple in red wine) crystals found in wines that have been subjected to very low temperatures. Either as a deposit or clinging to the cork. Crunchy and slightly acidic but harmless.
Thin As it suggests – dilute and lacking in flavour.
Tight knit As opposed to LOOSE KNIT – a firmly structured, usually concentrated wine with a multiplicity of well defined flavours – generally used of a wine which needs to soften.
Toasty Smell akin to fresh toast – associated mainly with OAKY white Burgundy and Chardonnay.
Tough A coarse texture due to ASTRINGENT TANNIN.
Tired Limp, feeble, lacklustre.
Trocken Literally "dry". German wines with up to 9 g/l of residual sugar.
Unbalanced One or more components unpleasantly lacking in, or dominating the flavour or texture of a wine.
Unctuous An almost too smooth, practically soapy texture.
Vanilla/vanillary The smell associated with wine that has aged in new oak casks, from the vanillin in the wood.
Vegetal Sometimes complimentary (mature red burgundy), often not: coarse, unpleasant smells of bruised or rotting vegetation.
Velvety Rich flavour, sumptuous texture.
Vendange tardive Mainly for wines from Alsace. Literally the same as the German *Spätlese*, i.e. late picked, but producing a much bigger and richer style of wine in Alsace; usually from Riesling or Gewürztraminer grapes.
Vigorous A full bodied wine which also has a firm acidity.
Vintage The harvest time, and also the year in which a wine was made.
Volatile Smelling of excess ACETIC acid (vinegar); a fault. (See OXIDIZED.)
Volatile acidity VA for short. Acetic acid (vinegar), called volatile because it smells, and in order to distinguish it from FIXED ACIDS which do not. VA is distinct from ACESCENCE, the smell of ETHYL ACETATE, though often associated with it.
Watery Low in alcohol, dilute in flavour.
Waxy One of the smells of mature Semillon and sometimes Chenin Blanc; partly an impression of texture as well.
Weak In structure: i.e. low in alcohol, acid and flavour.
Well balanced No element either lacking or unpleasantly obtrusive. In young wines needing time to mature, the constituent parts often stand out individually; but when the requisite proportions are correct, they may be described as well balanced, even though they are not yet married and HARMONIOUS.
Wet wool A smell associated with unoaked Chardonnay, particularly from Chablis, sometimes with young Semillon from Bordeaux.
Woody The impression of *old* wood on a wine – needs to be distinguished from OAKY = *new* wood. Not the same as CASKY which is a fault.
Yeasty The smell of active (i.e. fermenting) yeast, associated in a positive sense with Champagne and "sur lie" Muscadets, both of which have had prolonged contact with their yeast LEES.
Yield The amount of wine produced from a given area of vines. The less produced the more concentrated the wine will be. Too high a yield will make for dilute, watery wine.

INDEX